CAPITALIST GLOBALISATION, CORPORATED TOURISM AND THEIR ALTERNATIVES

CAPITALIST GLOBALISATION, CORPORATED TOURISM AND THEIR ALTERNATIVES

FREYA HIGGINS-DESBIOLLES

Nova Science Publishers, Inc.
New York

For permission to use material from this book please contact us:
Telephone 631-231-7269; Fax 631-231-8175
Web Site: http://www.novapublishers.com

NOTICE TO THE READER

LIBRARY OF CONGRESS CATALOGING-IN-PUBLICATION DATA

ISBN: 978-1-60692-112-8

Available upon request

Published by Nova Science Publishers, Inc. ✒ *New York*

CONTENTS

PREFACE

Any realistic understanding of contemporary tourism in the 21st century must be grounded in a context of the dynamics of capitalist globalisation. Sociologist Leslie Sklair's conceptualisation of capitalist globalisation and its dynamics as expressed in his "sociology of the global system" (2002) is employed to understand the corporatised tourism phenomenon and explain the resistance that it sparks. This discussion explains how a corporatised tourism sector has been created by transnational tourism and travel corporations, professionals in the travel and tourism sector, transnational practices such as the liberalisation being imposed through the General Agreement on Trade in Services negotiations and the culture-ideology of consumerism that tourists have adopted. These institutions, agents and processes have created a self-reinforcing system built upon growth dynamics and ever higher profit accumulation. This system reaps profits for industry and exclusive holidays for privileged tourists, but generates social and ecological costs which inspire vigorous challenge and resistance. Perhaps the most significant manifestation of this resistance is the coalition of the justice tourism movement which is seeking to replace the system of corporatised tourism with a more just, socially-concerned and sustainable tourism system. Such events suggest that the long-term future of tourism will be subject to macro-level tensions and challenges which forward-thinking tourism management will need to heed cautiously.

Chapter 1

INTRODUCTION

This book examines the topic of globalisation in order to establish a context for understanding the contemporary tourism sector. It begins by tracing how the conceptualisation of globalisation emerged from the modernisation and development discourse that characterised the twentieth century. The phenomenon of globalisation is then investigated by a brief exploration of the literature on globalisation in the economic, political and cultural arenas. This review reveals the complexity and multifaceted aspects of globalisation. However, concurring with the viewpoints of several analysts of globalisation (including Gill, 1995; McMichael, 1998; Sklair, 2002), it is proposed that it is capitalist globalisation that matters most because of its import and impact upon the contemporary global order. It will then be suggested that Sklair's analysis of the "sociology of the global system" (2002) with its focus upon the dynamics of capitalist globalisation offers a useful tool for analysing contemporary tourism in the current context of capitalist globalisation. This analysis focuses on the roles of individuals, institutions, transnational practices and the "culture-ideology of consumerism" in order to develop a comprehensive portrait of what is called "corporatised tourism". Like capitalist globalisation, corporatised tourism catalyses opposition due to its negative social and ecological impacts. Such dynamics suggest that the long-term future of tourism will be subject to macro-level tensions and challenges which forward-thinking tourism management will need to heed cautiously

Chapter 2

GLOBALISATION

2.1. THE EVOLUTION TO GLOBALISATION

The history of globalisation is contested by scholars (Holton, 1998) with some claiming an ancient pedigree while others view it as a more recent and modern phenomenon. Some analysts argue that globalising trends can be found in the earliest eras of human history (Frank 1996; Held, no date). Some refer to globalisation in its modern form and trace its development to the period of European colonisation beginning in the 1600s (Hoogvelt, 1997; Robertson, 1992). Other analysts however contend that globalisation has more recent roots. Stephen Gill in his discussion of globalisation as a "political project" (1999), sets its inception in the 1870s when the economies of North America and Europe pursued policies of the free flow of capital and a fixed exchange rate system based on the gold standard.[1] Although this system collapsed with the Great Depression (see Gill, 1999), it clearly demonstrated attributes of the interconnectedness of a globalised economy. However, it was only from the 1980s that globalisation took on its more potent and comprehensive form and came to the forefront of analysis. An understanding of contemporary globalisation must be grounded in its antecedents, the modernisation and development movements that characterised the period between the 1950s and the 1980s.

By the mid-twentieth century, the technological and economic achievements of key countries in Europe and North America, attained through the processes of

---

[1] This period could be called the first wave of globalisation. However, with his longer timeline, Robertson sees it as the third phase and calls it the "take-off phase" (1992, p. 54).

industrialisation,[2] led to a widespread acceptance of a modernisation perspective. According to Giddens:

> The key idea of modernisation theory is that the 'underdeveloped' societies remain trapped within traditional institutions, from which they have to break free if they are to approach the economic prosperity achieved in the West… 'underdevelopment' can only be overcome by the adoption of modes of behaviour based upon those found in existing industrialised societies (1986, p. 29).

Modernisation theory was based on a conceptualisation of progress that developed from 18th and 19th century rationalism that posited that if traditionalism were superseded by modernism with its technologies and efficiencies, then the economic benefits would accrue to other peoples.[3] Thus modernisation theory clearly set a global divide between the industrialised, "modern" states of the first or developed world and the yet to be developed states of the third or underdeveloped world. This marked the beginning of the development agenda which arose in the aftermath of World War II as the European colonisers struggled with their own rebuilding after the ravages of war, and the Americans rose to global power.[4]

Various voices have spoken out about more appropriate paths to development or have critiqued the developmental consequences of modernisation. One source of critique came from the dependency theorists who were influenced by Latin American structuralist thinking arguing that both external and internal structural forces led to developing countries being kept in a state of "dependency" within the international economic order (Todaro, 1997). Economist Andre Gunder Frank who was one of the founders of the dependency school of thought described the development project under modernisation as:

---

[2] In many European countries, such advances were based not only on industrialisation but also on the exploitation of the labour and resources of colonies which enabled the industrialisation process to succeed, an unacknowledged point among most proponents of modernisation.

[3] Cohen and Kennedy list key aspects of modernity that started in the 17th century and accelerated in the 18th and 19th centuries as "the growth of a questing spirit, a strong leaning towards the purposive pursuit of material and social 'progress', rationality, industrialization, urbanization and the triumph of the nation state" (2000, p. 378).

[4] Frank (1996) states that the support of the development agenda must be understood in the political context of the rise of American hegemony and concern with the spread of communism as the Chinese revolution followed upon the earlier Russian one. Frank claims "developing a more harmless alternative [to communism] became a matter of greatest urgency for the newly hegemonic United States" (1996).

Development became increasingly equated with economic development, and that became equated de facto if not de jure with economic growth. It in turn was measured by the growth of GNP per capita. The remaining 'social' aspects of growth [equals] development were called 'modernization'. Development meant following step by step in our (American idealized) footsteps from tradition to modernity (1996).

Following years of witnessing the effects of the "development" agenda particularly in Latin America but also in other areas of the developing world and trying to reconcile these with development theories, Frank posited a theory of the "development of underdevelopment". He argued that for developing countries "continued participation in the same capitalist world system could only mean continued development of underdevelopment" as their integration into the world economy was on capitalist terms and delivered the benefits to external investors (1996). As Britton succinctly described it: "'dependency' involves the subordination of national economic autonomy to meet the interests of foreign pressure groups and privileged local classes rather than those development priorities arising from a broader political consensus" (1982, p. 334). To avoid the pitfalls of dependency, some advocated autonomous development based upon import-substitution and nationally-driven industrialisation which has been described as "inward-oriented development" strategies (Brohman, 1996, p. 49). However, such strategies were subject to heavy fire from neoclassical economists who recommended developing countries concentrate not on developing their own industrial sectors but instead export primary commodities in a global trading network operating according to the market rules of comparative advantage (Brohman, 1996, p. 49). With the rise of neoliberalism and in particular the interventionist policies of structural adjustment of the IMF and World Bank, "outward oriented development" strategies have become the order of the day and almost all of the world's nations are tied into the global trading regime (Brohman, 1996).

While imperialism, modernisation, developmentalism and globalisation might be treated as entirely separate phenomena by some authors, Hoogvelt's study of globalisation characterises them all as interconnected phases of capitalist development and expansion (1997, pp. 16-17). Her typology sees four phases:

- 1500-1800 mercantile phase; transfer of economic surplus through looting and plundering, disguised as trade;
- 1800-1950 colonial period; transfer of economic surplus through 'unequal terms of trade' by virtue of a colonially-imposed international division of labour;

- 1950-1970 neo-colonial period; transfer of economic surplus through 'developmentalism' and technological rents;
- 1970- post-imperialism; transfer of economic surplus through debt peonage (Hoogvelt, 1997, p. 17).

Similarly, Waters views capitalism and modernisation as strongly interrelated:

> Capitalism... cloaks itself in the mantle of modernization. It offers the prospect not only of general and individual increases in the level of material welfare but of liberation from the constraints of tradition. This renders modernization as unavoidable and capitalism compelling (1995, p. 36).

This brief and cursory discussion indicates the heritage of globalisation from its antecedents of modernisation and development agendas. Prior to the era of modernisation, developing countries had viable traditional subsistence sectors even while many of them were tied into colonial trading regimes. With the advent of modernisation coinciding with the historical decolonisation movement, development became the key focus of concern as developing countries were urged to abandon traditional sectors, seek "development" and follow the model set by both European and American modernisers. Although dependency theorists challenged the viability and validity of the modernisation project and various paths to development were explored, including inward and outward development strategies, the rise of neoliberalism since the 1980s firmly geared developing countries to seeking development through engagement in external trading arrangements. This expanding network of global trading arrangements, as we shall see presently, has been one of the key drivers of the globalisation process.

2.2. PERSPECTIVES ON GLOBALISATION

It is perhaps arguable how globalisation came to the forefront of public discourse since the 1990s; including whether it was the development of "global" environmental consciousness of the "planetary environment" (Scholte, 2000, pp. 83-86; Waters, 1995, p. 103), the instantaneousness of communication achieved through the technology of the internet (Scholte, 2000, p. 74), the development of a global trading regime (Scholte, 2000, pp. 76-77) or all of these things. But since that time, globalisation has captured the attention of the public and academia.

Roland Robertson is a key contributor to the globalisation debate who argues that globalisation:

> ...refer[s] both to the compression of the world and the intensification of consciousness of the world as a whole...both concrete interdependence and consciousness of the global whole... (1992, p. 8)

As a result, Robertson sees the potential of globalisation as the possibility of the entire world becoming a single place. Similarly, Giddens claims:

> Globalization can... be defined as the intensification of worldwide social relations which link distant localities in such a way that local happenings are shaped by events occurring many miles away and vice versa (1990, p. 64).

Relevant transformations include: communications technologies such as the internet and satellite telephones which place distant regions in instantaneous contact; transportation technologies such as jumbo jets which facilitate globetrotting tourists and business people; financial systems allowing 24 hour global trading so that capital moves instantaneously and stock markets are constantly surveilled; and ecological impacts of global relevance including global warming and depletion of the ozone layer.

Gill argues that globalisation can be viewed as a set of trends:

> When most people hear the word 'globalization' they often think of a set of mega-trends and processes creating a more interlinked and integrated world. Phrases like 'the global village', 'the information society' and 'one world, ready or not!', all convey the sense that globalization is an accelerating, evolutionary process, where innovations in transport, science and technology, economics and communications increasingly link the fate and the future of humankind (1999, p. 1).

Scheuerman argues that although there is a diversity of perspectives on globalisation, "...most contemporary social theorists endorse the view that globalization refers to fundamental changes in the spatial and temporal contours of social existence..." such that the realm of the local and the utility of the nation-state are called into question (2002). Many definitions recognise that contemporary changes to the ways that humans relate in space and time have re-ordered our societies but beyond this, there is much variety in analysis. These differences reflect the various views on the sources, importance and the outcomes from these changes in spatial and temporal arrangements. Perhaps it is also indicative of the fact that there is a multiplicity of "globalisations"; as Giddens states "Globalization thus is a complex set of processes, not a single one. And these operate in contradictory or oppositional fashion" (1999, pp. 12-13). Three aspects or arenas of globalisation frequently partitioned and analysed include economic, political and cultural globalisation, which will now be briefly analysed.

2.3. THREE ARENAS OF GLOBALISATION

Perhaps one of the most pervasive perspectives on globalisation is the focus on the integration of the global economy. One of the leading analysts of *economic globalisation*, Kenichi Ohmae (1995), presents a business perspective on globalisation. He argues that globalisation results in the irrelevance of the state and the growth of regional powers such as the Chinese regional economy (potentially including not only the prosperous free trade zones of the Southeast coast and Hong Kong, but also Singapore and Taiwan) and the European Union. He views globalisation as the creation of a borderless world characterised by four flows: investment, industry, information and individuals (1995, pp. 2-4). He argues that states are no longer required to manage the market and that they must resist the urge to intervene (such as taxing prosperous zones for social redistribution) because if *laissez faire* policies are pursued the regional states can act as "engines of prosperity" (1995, p. 4).

It could be argued that the attempts to formulate global trade rules through such institutions as the World Trade Organization (WTO) and agreements such as the General Agreement on Trade in Services (GATS) and the failed Multilateral Agreement on Investment (MAI) are indicative of the formation of a wider economic globalisation. However, such a view has suffered setbacks since the United States, one of the main state drivers of economic globalisation, has resorted to conducting bilateral treaty negotiations with such countries as Australia, Chile and China following the opposition of developing countries to inequitable multilateral talks at the Cancun World Trade meeting in 2003. While multilateral talks in forums such as the WTO and GATS demonstrate advances in economic interdependency, global economic integration is a contested and complex matter in a world still driven by nation-states pursuing their own economic interests.

For analysts of *political globalisation*, one of the key concerns is the perceived receding role of the nation-state in a globalising world as the power of the nation-state is challenged in the management of its economy. As global trade expands, transnational corporations operate without the constrictions of borders, capital moves unrestricted and multilateral institutions such as the WTO organise macro-cconomic activitics. Correspondingly the powers, duties and roles of the nation-states in the global community become reduced and restricted. The extent and effectiveness of the "undermining of the state" is crucial in the wider globalisation debate because the institution of a truly global order, rather than a merely international one, necessitates a reduction in the political authority and effectiveness of nation-state actors.

Held and McGrew claim "the exclusive link between territory and political power has been broken" (2000, p. 11). A variety of factors make it apparent that politics is no longer confined within the borders of the territorial state. These include the development of international governmental organisations (IGOs) such as the United Nations and international non-governmental organisations (INGOs) such as Amnesty International; the development of international law through agreements and conventions such as the United Nations Convention on the Rights of the Child; developments of international authority above the powers of states such as the International Criminal Court; and the expansion of new social movements such that an international civil society could be said to be forming. According to Held and McGrew "in 1909 there were 37 IGOs and 176 INGOs, while in the mid-1990s there were nearly 260 IGOs and nearly 5,500 INGOs" (2000, p. 11). These IGOs and INGOs demonstrate webs of political action and interdependence that extend beyond state borders and challenge the sovereign authority of the territorial state.

Other analysts look to existing structures such as the United Nations at the international level and the European Union at the regional level and question whether they can be considered precursors to a global polity (e.g. Holton, 1998; Rosenau, 1996). The European Union provides the most advanced example of the willingness of states to surrender sovereignty to a larger political body but it remains a "work in progress" since clearly the roles of the member states have not yet been swept away despite efforts to share sovereignty. While some might see the United Nations as a potential precursor to "one world" government it is clearly currently a long way from serving as a global polity (see Holton, 1998). The United Nations is a complex umbrella institution which has structures of varying power and influence ranging from the Security Council with its executive capacities (though enfranchising only a handful of nation-states), to the General Assembly with its status as a "global forum", and specialised agencies such as the World Health Organization and UNESCO with their detailed concerns with various aspects of the global community including economic development, social justice, human rights and environmental issues (Holton, 1998, pp. 118-121).

Waters' judgement of progress in advancing political globalisation towards the achievement of a global polity is decidedly negative. He claims that political globalisation is strikingly less advanced than economic globalisation and its main advances have been in the areas of international relations and the development of political culture (1995, p. 122). However, Waters proposes that political globalisation is being facilitated by the more rapid development of *cultural globalisation* which fosters the development of common cultural values.

In fact, the cultural arena is one of the most important in the analysis of globalisation. The changes in temporal and spatial relationships between peoples and societies that are the foundation of globalisation mean that one must question the impacts on cultures[5] which develop organically within local and national contexts. Cultural homogenisation[6] refers to the tendency for contacting cultures to shed their differences under the influence of globalisation and to thereby become more alike. The ultimate concern that this arouses is the loss of cultural diversity and establishment of a monoculture, whether through cultural dominance as described by Westernisation and Americanisation or through cultural mixing as described by hybridity.

Cultural homogenisation arises largely from the obvious changes under way around the world as people join the market economy and adopt consumerism which challenges their traditional lifestyles. One particular discourse concerns westernisation. Theodore Von Laue focuses on what he calls the "revolution of westernization", which he describes as fostering a globalist vision (1987, p.109). He claims that the phenomenon of Western cultural forms spreading globally is due to Europe's historical advantage resulting from geography, the Greco-Roman cultural tradition and "the culture of cerebral asceticism" that sprang from Christianity and enabled Europe's development of science, technology and industry (p. 7). He claims that other peoples will not develop until they shake off their sensuality, become ascetic and develop ambition, or in effect become more "western". A more recent argument in a similar vein analyses the impacts of globalisation on culture and declares its "praise of cultural imperialism" (Rothkopf, 1997). Rothkopf advocates the nurturing of a global culture, and in particular, a global culture in the image of America's (which he describes as dynamic, tolerant and free), so that all will join in the global marketplace that works not only to American advantage but the world's as well. Similar to the discussion of modernisation, this discourse springs from the intellectual tradition

---

[5] Cohen and Kennedy claim "most sociologists tend to define culture as the repertoire of learned ideas, values, knowledge, aesthetic preferences, rules and customs shared by a particular collectivity of social actors. Drawing on this common stock of meanings enables them to participate in a unique way of life" (2000, p. 26).

[6] A related term that is important in the tourism literature is "acculturation", which refers to "...social processes and consequent social and psychological changes that occur when peoples of different cultures come into contact" (Nash, 2000, p. 6).

that supports Western penetration and transformation of other peoples and places. [7] In terms of the cultural homogenisation (as well as modernisation) thesis, what is demanded or lauded is that non-Western and underdeveloped peoples must transform themselves culturally to be like the West in order to achieve the successes and privileges enjoyed by their western neighbours. From this perspective, westernisation could be viewed as fostering such characteristics as individualism, consumerism, urbanisation, breakdown of familial ties, abandonment of tradition, secularisation and rationalism.

In a related vein, some analysts see globalisation as based on Americanisation. The historical backdrop for this position is the rise of American hegemony in the aftermath of World War II that coincided with the decline of British and European powers. Cohen and Kennedy describe this era as laying the foundations for a world society (2000, pp. 41-59) and note the important role of American economic power and political leadership as well as the promotion of English as the global language. Less measuredly, journalist turned globalisation analyst Thomas Friedman asserts:

> ...globalization has its own dominant culture, which is why it tends to be homogenizing to a certain degree...culturally speaking, globalization has tended to involve the spread (for better or worse) of Americanization – from Big Macs to iMacs to Mickey Mouse (2000, p. 9).

Friedman concludes after wide-ranging discussion and anecdotes from around the globe "...globalization is globalizing Anglo-American-style capitalism and the Golden Straightjacket. It is globalizing American culture and cultural icons. It is globalizing the best of America and the worst of America..." (2000, p. 380). While Friedman acknowledges that American-led globalisation has some detrimental impacts (and he does briefly address the need to ameliorate this), he is in effect a keen supporter of American-led, American-protected globalisation. As he makes clear:

> Sustainable globalization requires a stable power structure, and no country is more essential for this than the United States... the hidden hand of

---

[7]The westernisation position is countered by the discourse fostered by Edward Said's analysis of "orientalism" (1978). Said's legacy has been fruitful in fostering examination of cultural relativism, postcolonial studies, indigenist perspectives and offering support to feminist analysis. In a nutshell, Said argues that Western discourse asserts "otherness" as inferiority and thus legitimises cultural and other forms of domination. For a helpful discussion of Said's work in relation to cultural homogenisation see Holton 1998, pp. 164-166.

the market will never work without a hidden fist...America truly is the ultimate benign hegemon ...(2000, pp. 464 and 467).[8]

There is much criticism of the Westernisation and Americanisation positions. For example, referring to the Philippines, Appadurai argues that to claim it is subject to the forces of Americanisation is not accurate despite its long and close ties to the US. He sees:

> a confusion between some ineffable McDonaldization of the world and the much subtler play of indigenous trajectories of desire and fear with global flows of people and things... if a global cultural system is emerging, it is filled with ironies and resistances, sometimes camouflaged as passivity and a bottomless appetite in the Asian world for things Western (1996, p. 29).

Holton provides a balanced discussion on the strengths and weaknesses of the cultural homogenisation arguments and concludes "...the global field is multicentred rather than dominated by a single centre. There is no single dominant centre, in spite of the dominance of the USA [or West] or certain American symbols in particular markets or sectors..." (1998, pp. 169-170).

Hybridisation provides another important perspective on culture and globalisation. At its simplest, hybridity refers to the "...creation of dynamic mixed cultures" (Cohen and Kennedy, 2000, p. 363). It derives from anthropology and cultural studies and the related studies of syncretisation and creolisation which describe the way that cultures in contact serve as catalysts to change in each other.[9] Because of the intercultural mixing that globalisation fosters, hybridisation theory proposes that what results is "...cross-cultural borrowings and intercultural fusion and blending to create hybridized or mixed cultural forms" (Holton, 1998, p. 179). Of exceeding value here is Appadurai's examination of the global cultural economy in which he formulates his theory of flows of cultural objects that foster hybridity (1996). Appadurai uses the suffix "scapes" to designate these global flows and designated five of particular significance: ethnoscapes, technoscapes, finanscapes, mediascapes and ideoscapes.[10]

---

[8] Similarly, Rothkopf, referred to previously, advocates "exporting the American model" because "...of all the nations in the world, theirs is the most just, the most tolerant, the most willing to constantly reassess and improve itself, and the best model for the future" (1997, p. 47).

[9] Cultural syncretism is also a powerful argument against the Westernisation and Americanisation theses because both are in fact hybrid cultures that have drawn from the cultural, political and religious traditions of other civilisations that have preceded them sometimes by millennia.

[10] Ethnoscapes refers to the movement of mobile people such as tourists, businesspeople, migrant labour and refugees; technoscapes refers to the flow of technologies such as the internet, mobile

As the preceding discussion indicates, the globalisation literature indicates a wide breadth of analysis with much diversity in foci among the various analysts. Such a multiplicity of explanations of globalisation (or in line with Giddens (1999, pp. 12-13), "globalisations") could lead to confusion and abandoning the effort to pin down globalisation's importance to changes within our world.

2.4. IT IS CAPITALIST GLOBALISATION THAT MATTERS

While globalisation has a multitude of diverse forms that inspire much varied discussion and analysis, in terms of economic, social and environmental impacts, it is capitalist globalisation which arguably matters most. While people may be developing a "global consciousness", cultures may be undergoing hybridisation and technologies may be reducing time and spatial distances between societies and peoples, it is capitalist globalisation which is re-ordering individual lives, societies and world order in such a way as to create momentous tensions. These tensions are manifest in the devastating results that have followed the attacks of September 11, 2001 (Reid 2003, p. 3)[11] and environmental crises such as global warming which threaten the very future of the planet (Sklair, 2002, pp. 53-57). A number of analysts of globalisation have concluded after comprehensive review of globalisation literature that capitalist globalisation has more explanatory value if power, development, sustainability, social justice and equity are the concerns of discussion (Gill, 2000a, 2000b; Hoogvelt, 1997; McMichael, 1998; Scholte, 2000; Sklair, 2002).[12]

Development expert Philip McMichael in his article on "Demystifying 'globalisation'" argues that the debates to define and delineate globalisation are a "distraction" and that "that there is a more fundamental issue" to grapple with

---

phones and satellites which put distant peoples in contact; financescapes refers to the flows of capital globally; mediascapes refers to the global flows of information; and ideoscapes refers to the flows of ideas globally such as universal human rights and environmental awareness.

[11] Reid claims "While no one can condone the carnage of the events of September 11, they must be viewed as a rejection of corporate globalization and the exploitation taking place across the globe, and not simply as the actions of a few deranged individuals, as some would have us believe" (2003, p. 3).

[12] There are, of course, a number of other analysts who argue in favour of capitalist globalisation, including Norberg (2003) and Hoenig (2003). Their arguments suggest investment of capital in poor countries brings economic opportunities that would not otherwise occur. Their positions ignore the fact that such countries might have other economic options more beneficial to the welfare of their people and fail to address the equity concerns of the critics of capitalist globalisation. Many of these analysts belong to pro-market think tanks and media outlets. See: http://www.johannorberg.net/?page=indefense and http://www.moraldefense.com/default.htm.

(1998, p. 304). He claims that globalisation can be seen as a "historical project" which is about "managing power relations within states and across the state system" in order to secure a restructuring that works to secure market rule in the interests of "a powerful global managerial class" (1998, p. 304). The effects of this project are a diminution of the social agendas that all states were previously expected to pursue in meeting the needs of their peoples. For states of the developing world specifically, this meant abandoning their developmental agenda with its social aims, for a set of market criteria including efficiency, competition and entrepreneurialism that underline the agendas of market rule (McMichael, 1998).[13] Elsewhere, in his analysis of the WTO McMichael has argued that its "executive" activities in the support of market rule remove the development agenda from a public function of states to a private function of capital (2000, pp. 467 and 472). He claims that the WTO sends a message that "development now depends on the management of global markets" and the creation of a free trade regime with a result that "development becomes less a socially purposeful national initiative, and more a reward for joining the global market" (2000, p. 472). However, rather than being geared to deliver development to its member states such regulatory mechanisms as the trade regime of the WTO are meant "to facilitate corporate access to markets and raw materials, and investor and speculator access to financial markets, and to recalibrate the ideology of development as a global project" (McMichael, 2000, p. 473).

Jameson argues that the globalisation of the economy can be seen as a coerced integration:

> The rapid assimilation of hitherto autonomous national markets and productive zones into a single sphere, the disappearance of national subsistence (in food, for example), the forced integration of countries all over the globe into … that new global division of labour…[W]hat begins to infuse our thinking of globalization is a picture of standardization on an unparalleled new scale; of forced integration as well, into a world-system from which "delinking" (to use Samir Amin's term) is henceforth impossible and even unthinkable and inconceivable (2001, p. 57).

---

[13] McMichael states: "The globalisation project is premised on political-economic liberalisation of states. It subsumes the rhetoric of development and reconstructs it as efficiency, competition and entrepreneurialism. But it is not necessarily an equivalent project - it does not possess the coherence of the development project, anchored in the nation-building process. The latter was embedded, to a greater or lesser degree, in social goals specific to each state. The global regime has no social goals, just private/financial goals expressed in appeals to the abstract authority of the market" (McMichael, 1998, pp. 302-303).

Stephen Gill describes the contemporary form of capitalist globalisation as an attempt to impose a "neo-liberal market civilisation" (1995). He argues that this system includes culture, ideology and its own mythology of capitalist progress that has come about from the globalisation of neoliberalism. This ideology is put forward as the "sole model of future development" and is reinforced through the muscle of market discipline and political power (1995, pp. 399 and 412). He has coined two phrases to describe this coercive aspect to the system, "disciplinary neoliberalism" and the "new constitutionalism"; the former refers to the application of economic principles to all varieties of social relations and the latter describes the political-judicial structures being developed to secure the system's long-term future (2000a). Gill explains why such a theorisation of globalisation is merited:

> Whilst many authors have stressed the short-term perspectives with dominant forms of economic globalization, for example the sense of immediacy associated with time-space compression, the crucial strategic significance of new constitutionalism is how it seeks to provide political anchorage for the power of capital in the long term (2000a).
>
> Gill argues that it is this long term agenda of the new constitutionalism that matters as it brings about "deep structural transformations in economy, state and society" that will be difficult to overturn as they become "constitutionally" locked in (2000a).

Finally Sklair also concludes that it is global capitalism which matters most. After summing up a variety of approaches to understanding globalisation including world systems theory, the globalisation of culture model, the global polity and society model and global capitalism, Sklair claims that all such approaches can be faulted for their biases and limits (2002, p. 47). But on the latter approach, global capitalism, Sklair says that while it can be criticised as a "one-sided" approach, he suggests that two questions would remain vital to answer: just how important is that "one side"? And what problems does capitalist globalisation bring? (2002, p. 47). Considering his view that capitalist globalisation is irrevocably changing our world and bringing about major ecological and social crises, it is clear that Sklair thinks capitalist globalisation is worthy of concerted analysis. It is to his theory we now turn.

2.5. SKLAIR'S SOCIOLOGY OF THE GLOBAL SYSTEM

Sociologist Leslie Sklair has formulated an analysis of globalisation which has much to offer. Sklair describes his theory as a "sociology of the global system", which, although informed by the thinking of many other analysts of globalisation, was a radically new analysis when he first introduced it in his *Sociology of the global system* in 1991. In his later edition entitled *Globalization, capitalism and its alternatives* (2002), Sklair provides a valuable critique of what he calls capitalist globalisation and uses this as a springboard to contemplate an alternative globalisation that resolves the crises that capitalist globalisation produces. Sklair's model of globalisation is more holistic and comprehensive than most through his focus on transnational practices (TNPs) that encompass economic, political and cultural-ideological spheres (2002).

TNPs are the basis of the transcendence of national boundaries as countries become more bound together; they occupy the physical spaces of globalisation; they are present wherever transnational corporations (TNCs) are operating; members of the transnational capitalist class (TCC) meet and mingle and the culture-ideology of consumerism takes hold (2002, p. 86). Understanding how these TNPs contribute to the "capitalist project" requires examining the particular types of TNPs (economic, political and cultural-ideological) and then addressing how each TNP type is secured by its attendant structural form.

Economic TNPs refer to the economic practices that transcend state borders. This term encompasses a diverse range of phenomena ranging from export production to ethical trading regimes that are responses to the damages of export production practices. For Sklair's work which is primarily (though not exclusively) concerned with the effects of capitalist globalisation in the developing world, the key issue hinges around the capacity for economic TNPs to contribute to "development". Under the "capitalist project", the ideological assertion is that TNCs "...are the surest route to economic development on a global scale" (2002, p. 90). This is the reason many political and business leaders in the developing countries seek to entice TNCs to invest in their countries. However, the TNCs are not development agencies but profit-making enterprises that seek cheaper means of production and markets in which to sell their goods and services.[14] Sklair proposes that an investigation of TNCs' roles in providing jobs and economic linkages (both backward and forward)[15] within the host

---

[14] Therefore, they are not guaranteed to provide development but only opportunities for some well poised elites in those countries.

[15] Backward linkage refers to the situation when a TNC purchases local materials, goods or services in its production process thus stimulating development of local industries. In tourism, for

economy is a useful starting point to assess TNC contribution to development (2002, pp. 91-96). Sklair shows how the job creation/job destruction outcomes of TNC practice as well as the propensity or failure to create linkages within the economies where they locate, have the capacity to determine developmental outcomes and are thus some of the most important economic TNPs (p. 96). Following in-depth analysis, Sklair is led to conclude that the TNCs through their economic TNPs "...strive to control global capital and material resources..." (p. 115).

Political TNPs are political practices that transcend state borders. Sklair contends they are less advanced in today's world than economic TNPs due to the persistence of the state and attendant nationalisms (2002, pp. 96-98). However, the growth of civil society networks across borders indicate globalising tendencies as evidenced, for example, in the global proliferation of non-governmental organisations linked to environmental or human rights movements. What is of particular interest to Sklair is the advancement of political TNPs through the efforts of the transnational capitalist class (TCC) that is their structural promoter. According to Sklair, the TCC is composed of four "fractions": the corporate fraction composed of TNC executives and their local affiliates; the state fraction comprising globalising state and interstate politicians and bureaucrats; the technical fraction including globalising professionals; and finally, the consumerist fraction consisting of globalising merchants and media (Sklair, 2002, p. 99). According to Sklair, they are transnational in five aspects. They share both global and local economic interests; they seek economic control in workplaces, political control at all levels, and cultural-ideological control in everyday life; they hold global, not local, perspectives on a variety of issues; they are comprised of people from many nations all of whom partly identify as global citizens; and they share similar lifestyles predicated on luxurious consumption (2002, pp. 98-99). Sklair's formulation of the TCC argues that they are one coherent group whose mission is to secure the conditions under which their interests and the interests of the capitalist global system prevail at all levels from the local to the global (p. 99).

Cultural-ideological[16] TNPs are often identified as the driving force behind globalisation, whether characterised by other analysts as Americanisation, Westernisation (Barber, 1996; Holton, 1998; Von Laue, 1987) or

---

example, this would occur when a TNC hotel chain purchases locally grown farm produce or locally manufactured furniture. Forward linkage refers to the situation when TNC output goes into the local economy for further processing and thus adds value. An example is the manufacture of microchips for use in the production of locally produced consumer goods.

[16] Sklair places the two concepts "culture" and "ideology" together in this hyphenated form because he argues that capitalist globalisation is forging a "qualitatively new relationship" between these two previously distinct forces.

McDonaldisation (Ritzer, 1996). Cultural-ideological TNPs are manifest in such diverse phenomena as global communications through internet chatrooms, in concepts (consciousness) like McLuhan's "global village" (1962), in the spread of Western youth culture and in the development of a global environmental movement. However, it is how these TNPs manifest themselves under capitalist globalisation that is of interest to Sklair. Key to this is the structural form of the culture-ideology of consumerism which accompanies and promotes certain cultural-ideological TNPs (2002, p. 107). The culture-ideology of consumerism is a new phenomenon that has arisen due to the correlation of two simultaneous circumstances – the globalisation of capitalism and a powerful media, particularly the advertising industry, able to hail its bounties to everyone (p. 108). While consumerism is not new, the culture-ideology of consumerism is a distinct phenomenon as it promotes a consumerist "worldview". In effect, under capitalist globalisation, efforts of media and other agents of the culture-ideology of consumerism are geared toward controlling the "realm of ideas" in order to ensure that endless consumption underpins the whole of the capitalist system (Sklair, 2002, p. 115). As Sklair notes, the role of consumerism is the key - "without consumerism, the rationale for continuous capitalist accumulation dissolves" (p. 116). Its impact is tremendous as commercialisation and commodification is extended to every sphere of endeavour resulting in what Habermas terms "the colonization of the lifeworld" (cited in Sklair, 2002, p. 116). The idea that market dynamics are the most efficient dispenser of resources moves beyond the spheres of economic production into hospitals, schools, the community and homes. Neoliberal principles such as competition, individualism, an emphasis on "progress" and trust in technological solutions hold sway as a result. Table 1 provides an insight into the structures and processes that compose Sklair's articulation of the capitalist globalisation system.

One of the significant points of Sklair's analysis is that he admits that capitalism does deliver the goods, so to speak, at least to some in some places. The reason that the capitalist system has been able to be transplanted to the economies and societies of the Third and new Second worlds[17] is because the

---

[17] Sklair in particular addresses the experience of what he calls the Third World and the new Second World countries. This schematic is based on the "three worlds formula" proposed in the 1950s which divided the advanced, industrialised nations (First World) from the communist nations in Eastern Europe and the Soviet Union (Second World) and the "rest, the poorer and relatively unindustrialized, less developed countries" (Third World) (Sklair, 2002, p. 13). The new Second World acknowledges the changes wrought by the collapse of communist regimes following the fall of the Berlin Wall in 1989 but postulates that their status in development trajectories still necessitates a separate category. For a brief insight into this terminology and how its usage has changed see Holton, 1998, p. 12.

promise of development and the enticements of consumerism are desired and believed to be attainable by peoples and governments all around the globe. In fact the culture-ideological premises of capitalist globalisation are so successful, that to advocate other alternatives such as socialism brings contempt, dismissal and marginalisation. As Sklair states:

> The ultimate strength of capitalist globalization is that it continually works, and works very hard to persuade people that the system is natural, fair and fundamentally better than any realistic alternative (2002, p. 118).

Others have called this the "there is no alternative" syndrome [18] (Bennholdt-Thomsen and Mies, 1999, p. 52) which has been most effective at securing allegiance to the capitalist form of globalisation. Where this persuasion fails and opposition arises, capitalist globalisation has to date been effective in implementing strategies of coopting, countering or tarnishing the opposition. Capitalism's hegemony is underscored by the fact that it does not usually need to resort to force to achieve compliance. However, when force is required (as was the case for example at Genoa),[19] capitalism scores an even greater victory when the application of force is accepted as legitimate because it helps to underscore the legitimacy of the system (Sklair, 2002, pp. 118-119).

---

[18] Served by the acronym TINA, and supposedly originally stated by Margaret Thatcher. Some analysts of globalisation have been quick to counter the TINA syndrome for a variety of contradictory reasons. Those staffing international financial institutions such as the IMF and World Bank who are pro-globalisation but concerned at the increasingly vocal anti-globalisation fringe, argue that globalisation is reversible thereby threatening those that have a vested interest in the system but fail to advocate globalisation. Others who wish to raise the resistance and input of social movements to curb the excesses of globalisation oppose the TINA position in order to inspire activism (Hellyer, 1999; Wiseman, 1997). Those that are interested in challenging the proponents of the cultural imperialism thesis resist the TINA argument because their focus is upon cultural resilience in peripheral cultures and the phenomenon of hybridisation (Abu-Lughod, 1991; Lechner & Boli, 2000; Nederveen Pieterse, 2000; Sinclair, Jacka & Cunningham, 2000).

[19] This refers to the incident that occurred when "anti-globalisation" protesters gathered in Genoa, Italy in July 2001 to protest at the Group of 8's conference (the G-8 includes the industrialised nations of France, Germany, Russia, USA, Japan, Canada, Italy and Britain). Apparently, protester Carlo Giulani was shot in the head by police with live ammunition after he threw a fire extinguisher at a police vehicle. However, in the aftermath of these violent events, it has become more apparent that the Italian police were unnecessarily aggressive (for example using live bullets) in their tactics and that the violence of protestors was overstated. What is particularly interesting though for this discussion is how "Genoa" "…has become a kind of shorthand for 'violent protesters' in mainstream media" (see *Media missing new evidence about Genoa violence* at http://www.zmag.org/italy/missing_genoa_en.htm).

Current development orthodoxy encourages developing countries to integrate their economies into the global market as the best path to development.[20] Aspects of this process include seeking foreign direct investment, siting of TNC production in their locales, orienting economies to export-led production and implementation of IMF structural adjustment programs. For Sklair, it is important how each of these strategies serves capitalist globalisation.

Table 1. Sociology of the Global System (Sklair, 1999)

TRANSNATIONAL PRACTICES	LEADING INSTITUTIONS	INTEGRATING AGENTS
Economic sphere • Transnational capital • International capital • State capital	*Economic forces* • Global TNCs • World Bank, IMF • State TNCs	*Global Business Elite*
Political sphere • TNC executives • Globalising bureaucrats • Politicians and professionals • Regional blocks • Emerging transnational states	*Political forces* • Global business organisation • Open-door • Agencies, WTO • Parties and lobbies • EU, NAFTA, ASEAN, UN, NGOs	*Global Political Elite*
Culture-ideology sphere • Consumerism • Transnational • Neoliberalism	*Culture-ideology forces* • Shops, media • Think tanks, elite social movements	*Global Cultural*

---

[20] For example, the World Bank's website describes trade as: "vital for poverty-reducing growth". Accessed at: http://www.worldbank.org under "Issue Briefs">"Trade" (accessed on 23 April 2003). Also see: http://www.imf.org/external/np/exr/ib/2002/031502.htm in which the IMF advocates economic growth through globalisation of trade as the best hope for development in the developing world (accessed on 24 April 2003).

For example, on the issue of TNCs, Sklair states that like all businesses, TNCs seek profits (2002, p. 122). What is at issue is how they secure their profits. Radicals have criticised TNCs as exploitative of labour or as promoters of consumption, but that is only part of the picture. Under capitalist globalisation, TNCs' roles are supported by powerful agencies such as the World Bank and the IMF which advise countries to adopt policies that serve TNC interests; aid agencies fund programs implemented through TNCs in a way that aid seems to be more targeted to assist business than the poor; and TNCs bring with them a culture-ideology that transforms the society not only by introducing "business culture" into the economic sphere but also promoting consumerism to the wider society (Sklair, 2002, pp. 122-123).

Sklair states that to focus on the fact that TNCs exploit women, children or certain men (such as "men of colour") misses the point because capitalist production is based upon the exploitation of all factors of production (p. 131). Sklair emphasises that it is not the foreign origin of the firm that is at issue with TNCs; rather, what limits the developmental outcomes of TNC investment in developing communities is the nature of the product and the place held by production in that locality on the global commodity chain or as Sklair states "…its transnationality within the capitalist global system" (2002, p. 132). So the point is that some places in certain circumstances secure the benefits from TNC production that they seek and this explains why many developing country governments seek such investment.

This issue brings us to the problem of capitalist globalisation driven in particular by TNCs. Where focus is on the roles of TNCs operating in developing countries, concern is over trade.[21] However, a shift in focus to the goals of states who receive TNC investment, would prioritise development. The goals of states should be the developmental welfare of their peoples. However as Sklair demonstrates in his case study of the global food system, the priorities of capitalist globalisation lead to an emphasis on export production to meet the demand of wealthy consumers at the expense of subsistence production which feeds the poor (pp. 138-152). It is the results of these TNPs which lead to the paradoxical situation of Ethiopia designating land for export crops in the midst of a famine or Egyptian grain farmers being put out of business by American grain aid shipments (p. 145). As Sklair states, "the point at issue … is not whether a corporation and its practices are foreign, but to what extent they work in the interests of capitalist globalization … or in the interests of the majority of the

---

[21] Hence we have the debate on "free trade" versus "fair trade" as seen in the Oxfam engagement with the international financial institutions in their campaign entitled "Make trade fair" in 2002 (Oxfam International, 2002).

population" (p. 152). So while it is the business of TNCs to make profits and not to act as social charities, what we find under capitalist globalisation is that the spread of the market imperative means that governments whose responsibilities include supporting the social fabric, are undermined in this role by the agents of capitalist globalisation. This includes the IMF and the World Bank which impose structural adjustment programs (SAPs),[22] members of the TCC resident in a country who chant the mantra of the free market (including globalising politicians and bureaucrats) and the business elite including those working for the TNCs. While development could be achieved in many ways (such as endogenous, socialist or bureaucratic authoritarian development), the TCC works quite hard and has virtually succeeded in arguing that capitalist globalisation is the only vehicle to deliver economic growth and poverty alleviation.

However, there is another side to the developmental effects of capitalist globalisation in developing communities. In addition to the growth of TNC investment in Third World production gearing these countries to export production, there are the important effects of promoting the culture-ideology of consumerism in these same countries. Sklair notes that of all of the value systems that could be fostered in developing communities, capitalist globalisation serves to promote the culture-ideology of consumerism (2002). While debating whether consumerism versus producerism is the best path to development, Sklair argues that what is clear is that while consumerism may be difficult to connect to a state's developmental interest it is very easy to "… see how consumerism can be said to serve the interests of the capitalist global system" (p. 166).

> Capitalist globalization in the Third World depends on the successful promotion of the culture-ideology of consumerism among people with no regard for their ability to produce for themselves, and only with an indirect regard for their ability to pay for what they are consuming.[23] Development

---

[22] SAPs are programs pressed upon the governments of developing countries by such bodies as the IMF and World Bank in order to create the correct financial climate to secure international business investment in their economies. These programs include a mix of policies such as reduction in the public service sector, reductions in governmental social spending on health and education, privatisation of public assets such as electricity, communications and transport and financial deregulation. All these policies serve to integrate these countries' economies into the global economy, but Bennholdt-Thomsen and Mies argue that they effectively put the IMF and World Bank in charge of national economies (1999, p. 35). Such policies can strangle any true development at birth and leave the elites of the TCC to benefit from the market opportunities. They are now known as Poverty Reduction Strategy Papers (see http://www.imf.org/external/np/prsp/prsp.asp).

[23] This promotion of the culture-ideology of consumerism also occurs without any regard for the environmental effects or the effects on communities where some find themselves unable to secure the basic needs for survival (p. 166).

assistance (aid), for example, moves funds from taxpayers in rich countries to consumers in poor countries, but not always for appropriate forms of consumption, not to speak of what is siphoned off in corrupt deals or stolen. In this sense consumerism has nothing to do with satisfying biological needs, for people will satisfy these needs without any prompting from anyone else, but with creating what can be called induced wants (Sklair, 2002, p. 166).

These induced wants which are the mainstay of the culture-ideology of consumerism are generated in a number of ways, including what has been labelled cultural and media imperialism. What we find in this analysis, is that the promise of the new communications technologies is not turned to developmental purposes such as education as they were at first anticipated to do, but instead turned to the consumerist message of advertising. This may be in the form of entertainment such as television soap operas (which Sklair discusses as a vehicle for capitalist consumerism, p. 170), or advertising through cultural events through sponsorship agreements, or the association of a product with a lifestyle (for example the consumption of a cola drink evoking participation in (Western) youth culture).[24] Sklair assiduously avoids the debates that have embroiled those in cultural studies concerning the susceptibility of people in developing communities to advertising and media. Instead what he suggests is that rather than being dupes of this "media" or "cultural imperialism", people in developing communities are making rational choices which involve them in the consumerist project (2002, pp. 173-174). These consumerist products and experiences that they seek to purchase are attractive because they are cheaper than locally produced ones; they make life easier and/or they tap into symbolic power and meanings through their conferring of status and prestige (Sklair, 2002, p. 173).[25] While some rail against this as Americanisation or Westernisation, the fact is that capitalist globalisation will flog any commodity from any source that attracts buyers, and so we see not only Americana in demand but also products and experiences from around the globe -

---

[24] Sklair states: "There are few parts of the world in which the effects of the cola wars have not been felt. In even the most remote places Coke and Pepsi and their ubiquitous marketing slogans and logos are acknowledged as symbols of the American way of life. They are also marketed on the prospect that anyone, however poor, who can afford a bottle or a can, can join in the great project of consumerism, if only for a few moments" (2002, p. 196).

[25] It is in this section that Sklair examines Zayed's study of Cairo in which he notes that "Zayed's argument implies that once the culture-ideology of consumerism is adopted, poor people cannot cope economically, and a mode of resistance must develop. In the Muslim case this mostly manifests itself in religious extremism, whose target is as often Americanization as it is consumerism as such" (2002, p. 173). This is very informative in the aftermath of September 11, 2001 and the subsequent War on Terror. Unfulfilled consumerist ambition can lead to frustration manifesting itself in various forms of violence thereby creating a real threat of class polarisation discussed presently.

including world music, fusion cuisine, Tai Chi and Jackie Chan's martial arts films. Sklair contends that "...consumerism of capitalist globalization has a universal form but with the permanent potential of national-local cultural contents" (2002, p. 183).[26] He elaborates his theoretical discussion with four case studies in global consumerism[27] to illustrate two main points: one, that consumerism serves to promote consumption of non-essential products which may not be developmental, and can be deleterious or even deadly; and secondly, that capitalist globalisation serves to raise "... consumerist expectations that cannot be satisfied within the foreseeable future for billions of people around the world" (p. 204).

2.6. TWIN CRISES

Sklair argues that capitalist globalisation results in the creation of two crises[28] which bring with them the seeds for change. The first crisis is that of class polarisation which occurs both between and within countries and is manifested in a widening gap between rich and poor and an increase in the numbers of the very rich and the very poor (2002, p. 26). The state centric approach which argues that developed countries exploit developing countries misses the point; it is not location by birth that determines wealth status (there are very rich people in the developing world and very poor in the developed), but instead an individual's transnational class location (p. 26). The point of the polarisation crisis is that while capitalist globalisation promises to deliver development to all, its appropriation of resources through the mechanisms of the capitalist system delivers benefits to an elite minority associated with the TCC and often delivers debt, drudgery and even death to the majority populations. This can be simply

---

[26] This is particularly relevant to contemporary tourism.

[27] The four case studies include: the Nestle baby bottle feed controversy, the international effects of the pharmaceutical industry, the "cola wars", and the cigarette smoking industry.

[28] Sklair refers to the crises as the "two crises" however I like the implication of using the term "twin crises" for two reasons. One is the shadow that the attack on the "Twin Towers" of the World Trade Centre on September 11, 2001 casts upon globalisation and its "discontents". This has cropped up periodically within this text and which can be connected to the crisis of class polarisation in particular. Secondly the use of the term "twin" implies a relationship between the two crises, class polarisation and ecological unsustainability, which appears appropriate because these two phenomena are interrelated (for example, as evoked in the term "environmental racism" which describes how the impact of the environmental pollution burden falls inordinately upon the poor and people "of colour". See Haunani-Kay Trask (1993). However, these twins are admittedly more of the fraternal than the identical kind, because they address related but fundamentally distinct issues.

demonstrated by the disparities in access to education, safe drinking water, infant mortality, life expectancy, and other relevant statistics.[29]

The second crisis is that of ecological unsustainability. Capitalist globalisation is placing catastrophic demands on the natural environment through the overuse of resources to feed the insatiable appetite for continual growth and the generation of wastes and pollution in production processes. Both factors have generated unpredictable environmental change. Sklair asserts that the real issue is the role of the capitalist global system in these developments and not just the fact that modern economies naturally bring environmental degradation (2002, p. 56). At the heart of the problem is a capitalist system underpinned by a culture-ideology of consumerism which is geared to generate unsatiated consumerism and accumulation of goods which create unsustainability. While the ideology of capitalism advocates the ability of human science and technology to mitigate these problems, and in particular the concept of sustainable development assures us we can manage these issues, at the heart of capitalist globalisation lies an ecological crisis which is intrinsic to the system.

The twin crises give rise to challenges to globalisation as opponents strive to bring down the capitalist global system. Elements of the anti-capitalist globalisation movement logically come from the various components of the green movement who oppose the effects of capitalist globalisation on the environment, and from the labour movement concerned by the advent of class polarisation wrought by the same forces. However, these two factions are joined by numerous other individuals, organisations and communities motivated by their concern with the effects of capitalist globalisation, be it a narrow issue such as endangered species or export-processing zones, or broader issues such as human rights and sustainability. The proponents of capitalist globalisation, most notably the TCC, recognise the threat that the various factions of the "anti-globalisation" movement represent and have sought to limit their impacts through usurping the sustainability debate through the conceptualisation of sustainable development

---

[29] For insights, see *The world guide 2005-06* (New Internationalist, 2005) and the World Bank group's *World development report* at: http://econ.worldbank.org/wdr/. While some might assert that these disparities are not the key issue as development has improved the welfare of people in the developing world to a level that otherwise would not have occurred, others contend that glaring poverty is unacceptable in a world with sufficient resources to relieve the material needs of all. For instance see Kostigen (2004) and Cooper (2005) for arguments about how the "wealth gap" is a key issue even in rich societies such as the USA and UK. Kostigen provides the statistics of Third World poverty and argues that "in just 14 days the problems of the poorest countries in the world - starvation, lack of education, scarcity of potable water, etc. - could be solved if each nation donated its military spending budget for just that period of time - 14 days" (2004).

and co-opting major players in the green movement.[30] Nonetheless, opponents of capitalist globalisation have explored a variety of alternatives.

Sklair devotes some attention to one group of reactions that can be characterised as "de-linking" from the global system (or localisation) which are evidenced in initiatives like the Local Exchange Trading Systems (LETS), permaculture networks and slow food movements. He claims that these represent an alternative to globalisation but not to capitalism as capitalist globalisation "...could accommodate and subvert most of these initiatives and turn them into variations on the consumerist theme" (2002, p. 285).[31] Because the twin crises are not resolvable within capitalism, Sklair advocates an agenda that involves moving forward towards globalisation without capitalism (p. 299). Sklair argues widespread transformation is necessary as reform of capitalist globalisation will not resolve the twin crises. He states "because I cannot accept the optimistic hope that capitalism can become much more humane globally than it already is...in my view the next step in the quest for human progress has to be the transformation of capitalist globalization into socialist globalization through the globalization of human rights" (2002, p. 324).

2.7. TOWARDS SOCIALIST GLOBALISATION

In addressing the alternatives to capitalist globalisation, Sklair suggests that the conditions that capitalist globalisation create actually enable circumstances that give rise to socialist globalisation. These include not only whipping up opposition to capitalist globalisation as a result of the damages of the twin crises, but also the interconnectedness that capitalist globalisation has created, the development of shared cultural values centred on human rights and the attainment of a certain level of affluence that makes the socialist alternative possible. While capitalist globalisation opens up the material opportunity for socialist globalisation in this way, it tries to shut down avenues to it in the political and ideological spheres (Sklair, 2002, p. 27). For Sklair the key criterion for judging

---

[30] Sklair in particular discusses how the corporate leaders "captured" the 1992 Earth Summit at Rio. As a result much of the sustainable development debate remains embedded within the market paradigm so that the connections between the environmental crises of our time and the culture-ideology of consumerism which engender them are never overtly linked (Sklair, 2002, p. 276

[31] This tendency for capitalist globalisation to subvert alternative movements is paralleled in tourism where, for instance, the tourism industry is accused of subverting alternative tourisms for profit and public relations (see Wheeller, 1991).

capitalist globalisation is whether it can deliver global, equitable development and he categorically denies that capitalist globalisation can deliver on these promises:

> While capitalism may be the only system that can produce plenty, theory and practice suggest that it cannot distribute it fairly on a global scale, that is capitalism cannot develop the Third World (1994, p.181).

How would socialist globalisation come about and what would it look like? Sklair advocates a path to socialist globalisation through the creation of true cooperative democracies which would provide a transition and allow the creation of a culture of human rights (2002, pp. 300-321). In contrast to the capitalist global system predicated on a culture of consumption, the socialist global system underpinned by the culture of human rights would set values around realisation of sustainability, social justice and equity and not accumulation of material possessions.[32] People would still consume but it would not be through the exploitative use of the environment and the labour of others that the current system fosters. Emphasis would not be on never-ending, compulsory and compulsive consumption but on an adequate standard of living. Sklair's conceptualisation argues that the currently accepted notion of universal human rights being limited to those of the civil and political kinds would have to be expanded to add as equally valuable and protected those economic and social rights currently relegated as second-tier rights (2002, pp. 306-311).

While Sklair acknowledges that his vision of socialist globalisation could be regarded as utopian, he argues that one can visualise its achievability by examining how the seeds of socialist globalisation can be built on the foundations of present circumstances (p. 305). To this end he examines producer-consumer co-operatives (P-CCs)[33] as an alternative to the TNCs, a culture of human rights

---

[32] Consumerism under capitalist globalisation promises the consumerist vision of the good life on an individualistic basis. The ideology promises that if an individual will join the capitalistic system as worker and consumer, the bounties of fulfilment will flow their way whether it be the small tangibles of a can of coke, the more intangible freedom evoked by the Marlboro cigarette or the big tangibles of BMWs and holiday homes. On the other hand, socialist globalisation seeks to secure the good society on a collectivistic basis, where through the adherence to human rights values, all will be guaranteed an adequate quality of life and the peril of the twin crises can be avoided.

[33] P-CCs are market structures which place producers (sometimes worker-owned enterprises) and consumers in social as well as economic relationships and do not privilege profits over fair wages for workers, environmental sustainability and health of consumers. A well known example is the Mondragon network of cooperatives in Spain. These enterprises have the social connectedness that fosters social responsibility that TNCs lack. Sklair states that the contemporary principles of stakeholder theory which form part of current discussions of

(the full range mentioned above – economic, social, political and civil) as a replacement for the culture-ideology of consumerism and a political system based on political transnational practices of the P-CCs "…entering into larger political and/or economic units on the basis of genuine decision-making, not the transnational capitalist class focused on the organizing of the global system for private profits" (p. 305).

Sklair states that while socialist globalisation is just one alternative to capitalist globalisation, pursuit of an alternative is not optional because of the catastrophe that looms as a result of the twin crises linked to capitalist globalisation which it is unable to resolve. Sklair concludes:

> What capitalist globalization fails to provide are genuine opportunities for people to make their own choices about whether to live in a forever increasingly marketized society where fewer and fewer things and experiences escape commercialization. While the culture-ideology of consumerism provides ever-expanding apparent choices of goods and services, there is little or no choice about whether or not we wish to live in the consumerist lifeworld. Capitalism takes the global system to the level of material abundance for some, but unrestrained consumerism creates environmental degradation and resource scarcity and still fails to raise the living standards of all to anything like a satisfactory degree. Socialist globalisation would eventually raise the quality of life (rather than the standards of living set by consumerist capitalism) of everyone and render the culture-ideology of consumerism superfluous by establishing less destructive and polarizing cultures and ideologies in its place. There is no blueprint for this – if we want such a world we will have to create it by trial and error (2002, p. 325).[34]

Sklair's work addresses much of the vast terrain that is globalisation. His critique of capitalist globalisation has been the focus of much of his life's work and has made important contributions to the understanding of the material effects of this phenomenon. Equally important is his objective of providing a normative

---

corporate citizenship reflect relationships that P-CCs would create and represent what could be characterised as socialist practice within capitalist societies (2002, p. 302).

[34] While sounding utopian, we can see some of the changes advocated by Sklair presently occurring in Argentina as a result of the 2001 economic crisis during which market relations disintegrated and people turned to worker-run cooperatives, barter arrangements and community solidarity networks to meet their needs. Dangl (2005) provides an analysis of two case studies, the Hotel Bauen and the Chilavert book publishing factory, which illustrates possible alternatives to the dynamics of capitalist globalisation. It is also visible in the changes underway in Venezuela where under Hugo Chavez, "Endogenous Development Zones" are encouraging workers cooperatives in such areas as manufacturing, agriculture and tourism (see Harnecker, 2006, p. 11)

consideration of globalisation's alternatives following in the footsteps of numerous others (e.g. Cohen and Kennedy, 2000; Henderson, 1999; Hoogvelt, 1997).

Sklair's work provides a sound foundation to explore contemporary tourism. However, there is one deficiency in Sklair's analysis to be rectified before proceeding to this. While the culture-ideology of consumerism does much to explain how capitalist globalisation perpetuates itself through making consumers of everyone, it is not enough. It provides one side of the equation as to how capitalist globalisation obtains the support of people everywhere despite the fact that it fails to deliver the goods that it promises to everyone. However, it fails to emphasise the other side of the equation that is alluded to in Sklair's use of the term "global capitalist project" (2002, p. 46). The global capitalist project is the assertion of political power which secures capitalist globalisation and is underpinned by the ideological assertion that capitalist globalisation is the only viable organising system at the global level which will deliver prosperity and freedom to all. Stephen Gill has provided valuable insights into this aspect of globalisation (1995, 1999).

Gill's (1995, 1999) analyses focus on the "market fundamentalism" [35] of "market civilisation"[36] which is undergirded by "disciplinary neoliberalism".[37] He contends that "the dominant forces of contemporary globalisation are constituted by a neoliberal historical bloc that practises a politics of supremacy within and across nations" (1995, p. 402). He characterises this as an attempt to impose a "neo-liberal market civilisation" that includes not only prescribed economic structures, but also a culture, ideology and its own mythology of capitalist progress that has come about from the globalisation of liberalism. This ideology is put forward as the "sole model of future development" and it is reinforced through

---

[35] This is a very evocative term as it has the connotation of religious fundamentalisms and implies that faith in the god-like powers of the market advocated by the supporters of market civilisation is as uncritically promoted as Islamic or Christian fundamentalist beliefs.

[36] Gill introduces his concept of market civilisation in the following terms: "The present world order involves a more 'liberalised' and commodified set of historical structures, driven by the restructuring of capital and a political shift to the right. This process involves the spatial expansion and social deepening of economic liberal definitions of social purpose and possessively individualist patterns of action and politics... capitalist norms and practices pervade the *gestes repetes* of everyday life in a more systematic way... so that it may be apposite to speak of the emergence of what I call 'market civilisation'" (1995, p. 399).

[37] This presents a discourse of governance which "...stresses the efficiency, welfare, and freedom of the market, and self-actualisation through the process of consumption" and it promotes "...policies that tend to subject the majority to market forces whilst preserving social protection for the strong (e.g., highly skilled workers, corporate capital, or those with inherited wealth)" (1995, p. 401).

the muscle of market discipline and political power (1995, pp. 399 and 412).[38] Gill
notes that while market forces have been part of human society for eons, "…it can
be argued that a disturbing feature of market civilization is that it tends to generate
a perspective on the world that is ahistorical, economistic, materialistic, 'me-
oriented', short-termist, and ecologically myopic" (1995, p. 399). Similar to
Sklair's "capitalist project", Gill argues that:

> New constitutionalism is a macro-political dimension of the process
> whereby the nature and purpose of the public sphere … has been redefined in
> a more privatised and commodified way…the new constitutionalism can be
> defined as the political project of attempting to make transnational liberalism,
> and if possible liberal democratic capitalism, the sole model for future
> development. It is therefore intimately related to the rise of market
> civilisation (1995, p. 412).

Gill's reflections offer a more strident emphasis on the aspects of political
power that play out in capitalist globalisation which is less evident in Sklair's
"culture-ideology of consumerism" concept. Together, Sklair's culture-ideology
of consumerism and Gill's market fundamentalism provide a fuller picture of how
capitalist globalisation asserts its hegemony via persuasion and coercion. Sklair's
and Gill's analysis can be effectively employed as a tool to understand the
contemporary dynamics of global tourism. Such an analysis suggests that
capitalist globalisation and a globalised tourism industry have formed a symbiotic
relationship of significant importance.

---

[38] Gill frequently calls this phenomenon "the new constitutionalism" and "disciplinary neoliberalism"
     (1995).

Chapter 3

FROM GLOBALISATION TO CORPORATISED TOURISM

The preceding section investigated globalisation and proposed that, because of its significant impacts, it is capitalist globalisation that "matters most". The dynamics of this system analysed by Leslie Sklair in his "the sociology of the global system" provides a model against which the processes of contemporary tourism can be analysed (2002). This section takes up this task by focusing on the transnational practices of contemporary tourism, the institutional structures and organisations which are effective, the roles of the transnational capitalist class and its various "fractions" in tourism and the culture-ideologies operative in its conduct. The question will then be explored: to what extent do Sklair's "twin crises" of class polarisation and ecological collapse apply to the tourism sector. Lastly, Sklair's proposition of an alternative to capitalist globalisation begs the question: is there an alternative to corporatised tourism that might contribute to avoiding the impending "twin crises"?

3.1. CONTEXT OF THE GLOBAL TOURISM INDUSTRY

While some promoters of tourism such as the World Travel and Tourism Council (WTTC) describe it as the world's biggest industry, this claim is open to some challenge and debate.[39] However, the relevant statistics fully confirm that it

---

[39] Pleumarom calls it "the self-proclaimed biggest industry" (no date b), perhaps concurring with the conclusion of Leiper (1995) that tourism advocates are exaggerating its size and import in order to gain political influence.

is a force of increasing global significance. In 2003, international tourism receipts represented approximately 6 per cent of worldwide exports of goods and services (as expressed in US$) according to the United Nations World Tourism Organization (UNWTO, no date a). If service exports are analysed exclusively, the share of tourism exports increases to nearly 30 per cent of global exports (UNWTO, no date a). Tourism is credited with creating more than 234 million jobs worldwide – almost 9% of the world's workforce (WTTC, no date a). Forecasting by bodies such as the UNWTO and the WTTC predicts extraordinary growth in tourism. For instance, the UNWTO's *Tourism 2020 vision* forecasts that international arrivals are expected to reach over 1.56 billion (the current volume being 694 million) by the year 2020 and

> East Asia and the Pacific, South Asia, the Middle East and Africa are forecasted to record growth at rates of over 5 per cent per year, compared to the world average of 4.1 per cent. The more mature regions Europe and Americas are anticipated to show lower than average growth rates. Europe will maintain the highest share of world arrivals, although there will be a decline from 60 per cent in 1995 to 46 per cent in 2020 (UNWTO, no date b).

With globalisation as the focus of attention, analysts tend to concentrate on international tourism. However, it should not be forgotten that domestic tourism is by far the larger phenomenon with about 80% of tourist trips coming from the activities of domestic tourists (Cooper, Fletcher, Fyall, Gilbert and Wanhill, 2005, p. 4). While the majority of this domestic tourism is within the wealthier nations of the OECD, some of the wealthier countries of the developing world also have significant domestic tourist sectors including Mexico, Thailand, China, India, Brazil and South Africa.[40] In addressing international tourism, it must also be recognised that the majority of tourists originate from and travel between developed countries (Harrison, 2001, p. 10). However, the place of developing countries in global tourism is worthy of focus because as Harrison argues, it is clearly evident that tourism to the less developed countries (LDCs) is "significant and increasing", with 1997 seeing 30% of international arrivals and 30% of

---

[40] Interesting statistics on this phenomenon include the fact that in 1995, 75% of hotel patrons in Mexico were domestic visitors; in Thailand there were 42.5 million domestic trips compared to 7.4 million international tourists trips; and in 1999 Chinese domestic tourists accounted for 90% of total tourism and 70% of revenue (UNWTO, 2002b, p. 19). David Goldstone (2005) has written a much needed and valuable analysis of the nature, size and importance of domestic tourism in developing countries with a particular focus on Mexico and India.

international tourism receipts occurring there (Harrison, 2001, p. 11).[41] Under the logic of the neoliberal system, development is meant to be achieved by embracing the global market and focusing upon exporting. Thus engaging in international tourism is now seen as one of the most important paths to development for developing countries as it is an export activity. When one considers that the majority of international tourists to the developing world originate from the developed countries (Harrison, 2001, p. 11), one can see how concerns with associated structures of globalisation and issues of social justice become very relevant contexts for discussion.

3.2. GLOBALISATION AND TOURISM

That tourism is an ideological phenomenon should not be underestimated.[42] The following quote by a representative of the TCC Conrad Hilton illustrates this point when he claims "each of our hotels is a little America" and "we are doing our bit to spread world peace, and to fight socialism" (cited in Crick, 1989, p. 325). Translated into the current context, Hilton and his cohorts in the TCC might claim that their hotels and businesses are doing their bit to spread market ideology and consumerism. Previously, Friedman was quoted as stating "…globalization is globalizing Anglo-American-style capitalism and the Golden Straightjacket" (2000, p. 380). Hilton's observation infers that tourism has its role to play in this endeavour. This is why the proposition that tourism might serve as an ideological support for the advance of capitalist globalisation is worthy of further exploration.

The symbiosis that has formed between tourism and capitalist globalisation is one of the defining features of our era. Some analysts of globalisation have attempted to explore the nature of this relationship and analyse its effects. Cohen and Kennedy argue that "… international tourism has an outreach greater than other powerful globalizing forces, even TNCs" (2000, p. 213). Considering tourism's scope, volume, organisation and impacts, they observe that:

> It is possible to argue that tourism may also exercise a cumulative effect that is considerably greater than any other single agent of globalization. While a similar claim has been made about TNCs, which have rightly been

---

[41] Diaz-Benavides provides some very useful statistics and insights into the impacts of tourism on the least developed countries (LDCs) in the late 1990s, notably that almost 24% of world tourism revenues in 1999 went to developing countries and for at least one-third of developing countries (and 24 of the LDCs), tourism is the main source of export income (2002).

[42] Hall (2003) argues that the political nature of tourism has largely been either neglected or ignored within mainstream tourism research.

seen as carriers of technology, capital and the 'culture-ideology of consumerism' (Sklair 1995: 147), the numbers of TNC personnel who move in order to work in foreign countries is quite small. Moreover, their operations normally require or encourage relatively few individuals to engage in direct, face-to-face social interactions across national boundaries (Cohen and Kennedy, 2000, pp. 213-214).

Similarly, Wahab and Cooper assert "tourism is at the forefront of the creation of a global society" (2001b, p. 319). Lanfant and Graburn have claimed:

> International tourism is not just an international extension of domestic tourism, nor just a major contribution to foreign exchange, but it is also a 'transmission belt' connecting the developed and underdeveloped worlds. Tourism policy has become part of a global project which lumps together seemingly contradictory economic interests: the organization of vacations (an idea originating in rich countries) and the aspirations for development of economically weak societies (1992, pp. 95-96).

Pleumarom charges that tourism is one of the most competitive and centralised industries and that "hardly any other economic sector illustrates so clearly the global reach of transnational corporations" (1999b, p. 5).[43] In fact such dynamics has resulted in a corporatised tourism sector which is defined by its adherence to the values of capitalist globalisation.

Britton's work (1982) using dependency theory to explain the dynamics of international tourism is vital to any analysis of how contemporary tourism and contemporary globalisation support and reinforce each other. He succinctly describes the international tourism hierarchy operating in developing country contexts: at the top are the large tourism corporations of the "metropolitan market countries"; in the middle are the "branch offices and associate commercial interests of metropolitan firms operating in conjunction with their local tourism counterparts" in the developing country; and lastly, there are the small to medium enterprises (SMEs) of the developing country which are dependent on the middle layer but marginal to their interests (1982, p. 343). Thus we see that the international tourism trade is based upon an inequitable structure and this is what

---

[43] However, it must also be recognised that the vast majority of tourism enterprises around the globe are small to medium enterprises (see Fayos-Solá & Bueno, 2001, p. 55). However, while proportionally smaller in numbers, the issue is the power that the large TNCs can exert to shape the operations of the tourism industry in their interest.

creates the imbalanced outcomes of international tourism in a global capitalist economy.[44] Britton explains:

> The degree of penetration by foreign capital, or conversely, the extent of a colony's incorporation into the global capitalist economy, is the most important cause of structural distortions. A form of economic growth (not 'development') is encouraged which, through 'spin-offs' and 'trickledown effects,' marginally improves absolute per capita standards of living. But it does so in a way that overwhelmingly transfers the great proportion of accumulated capital and welfare benefits to ruling classes and foreign interests (1982, p. 348).

The United Nations Conference on Trade and Development (UNCTAD) has also voiced concerns about these issues as it has argued that the "trickledown" impacts of tourism are negated by "the predatory practices and anti-competitive behaviour" of the big tourism operators in developing countries (cited in Vivanco, 2001). This results in financial leakages (loss of foreign exchange through purchase of imports to supply tourists) and unbalanced and unfair trade outcomes.

In fact, Britton's analysis of the experience of states in the Pacific Islands indicates that incorporation into the global tourism system correlates with past colonisation by a metropolitan power. This suggests that capitalist exploitation through tourism is a continuation of the dynamic of colonial exploitation to extract surplus wealth.[45] McLaren has argued more recently that "tourism increases local reliance upon a global economy" (1998, p. 17). It does this by undermining subsistence living; promoting the accumulation of debt to construct the infrastructures and facilities that tourists require; relying on foreign investment and commercial presence; requiring products and services from outside the local economy and by psychologically drawing locals into the culture-ideology of consumerism.[46] Burns (1999, p. 132) reminds us that unlike in the developed world, tourism in developing countries does not usually evolve from natural

---

[44] For a more recent exposition applying dependency theory to mass tourism development, see Khan (1997).

[45] Hall and Tucker (2004) have edited a volume of works investigating the relationship between tourism and postcolonialism which suggest that colonial patterns of exploitation and dependency still resonate in contemporary tourism.

[46] On this latter point, Pleumarom argues that one factor in the Asian economic crisis of the late 1990s, was that many Asians imitated tourists in a "free-spending frenzy" on luxury goods. The result in Thailand was an unleashing of "greed and consumerism [that] devastated whole communities" (1999b, p. 7). Such behaviour has been eloquently described as "injecting the behaviour of a wasteful society into the midst of a society of want" (Boudhiba cited in Crick, 1989, p. 317).

economic and social processes in these countries and it is for this reason tourism is frequently accused of being an imposed and exploitative force.

The role of institutional structures in promoting the dynamics of corporatised tourism should not be underestimated. Britton argued over two decades ago that "The World Tourism Organization, International Monetary Fund, United Nations, World Bank and UNESCO, among others, set the parameters of tourism planning, promotion, identification of tourism products, investment and infrastructure construction policies often in conjunction with metropolitan tourism companies" (1982, p. 339). It is these institutions which establish the structures that foster the growth and development of the international tourism industry and in effect support the wider development of capitalist globalisation. Some of these institutions will now be examined in greater detail in order to see how they might support the processes of capitalist globalisation as described by Sklair (2002).

3.3. INSTITUTIONS

3.3.1. The World Tourism Organization

One of the most prominent institutions in any consideration of international tourism is the World Tourism Organization (UNWTO). [47] In 2005, it had a membership of 145 states, seven territories and more than 300 Affiliate Members from the public and private sector (UNWTO, no date a). This organization has a very tall mandate; it is a specialised agency of the United Nations entrusted with

> promoting the development of responsible, sustainable and universally accessible tourism, with the aim of contributing to economic development, international understanding, peace, prosperity and universal respect for, and observance of, human rights and fundamental freedoms. In pursuing this aim, the Organization pays particular attention to the interests of developing countries in the field of tourism (UNWTO, no date a).

---

[47] Formerly, the World Tourism Organization used the acronym WTO-OMT to distinguish it from the World Trade Organization which used the acronym WTO-OMC (the former signifying World Tourism Organization-*Organisation mondiale du tourisme* from the latter World Trade Organization-*Organisation mondiale du commerce*). However, in 2005 when the World Tourism Organization became a specialised agency of the United Nations, the acronym UNWTO was adopted to avoid confusion between these two international organisations; the World Trade Organization now uses the acronym WTO.

The UNWTO has a very long history as an international organisation. It began as the International Union of Official Tourist Publicity Organizations in 1925 based at The Hague and became the International Union for Official Tourism Organizations (IUOTO) in 1949 with a move to Geneva. These were both technical, non-governmental organisations whose members included 109 National Tourism Organisations and 88 Associate Members from both the public and private sphere (UNWTO, no date a).

However, the 1960s saw significant changes that impacted upon this organisation. Tourism had developed into a major phenomenon and became increasingly international in character. As a result in 1967, IUOTO members passed a resolution to transform the organisation into an inter-governmental organisation with a mandate to deal with tourism issues on a global scale and able to liaise with other relevant organisations, including such bodies of the United Nations as the World Health Organization (WHO), UNESCO and the International Civil Aviation Organization (UNWTO, no date a).

In 1975 the IUOTO was renamed the World Tourism Organization and made its headquarters in Madrid on the invitation of the Spanish government. In 1976 the UNWTO became an executing agency of the United Nations Development Programme (UNDP) and in 1977, it signed a formal agreement of cooperation with the United Nations.

The change in the 1960s to make the UNWTO an inter-governmental organisation rather than stay as a non-governmental organisation reflected the realities of modern tourism as it became a significant economic sector in many countries. The UNWTO on its website refers to "the unstoppable growth of tourism" (no date a), resulting in it becoming one of the most important industries in the world. This economic power, coupled with the environmental and social impacts that can accompany uncontrolled mass tourism indicates the necessity of having governments at the forefront of international tourism policy. In 2003, the UNWTO became a specialised agency of the UN. The Secretary General of the UNWTO, Francesco Frangialli, stated this would

> constitute a remarkable step forward, which can be characterized by three words: recognition, effectiveness, and impetus. Recognition, because it acknowledges the fact that travel, leisure and tourism constitute a powerful part of modern society that cannot be ignored. Effectiveness, because, due to tourism's multidisciplinary nature, many agencies and organs of the system are involved in its expansion in the performance of their own specific responsibilities. Transforming the WTO [UNWTO] into a specialized agency would mean greater coherence by increasing the synergies among those different stakeholders and enhancing the coordination carried out by

ECOSOC. And impetus - because we expect to achieve greater visibility that would prompt governments as well as multilateral institutions, especially the Bretton Woods institutions, to pay increased attention to an industry that brings development (UNWTO, 2002a).

This quote indicates one of the most significant roles that the UNWTO plays, which is to serve as a "booster" for the stature and recognition of the tourism industry. As part of this effort, the UNWTO has programs focused on the statistics and measurement of the tourism industry.[48] Such an effort effectively emphasises the importance of economic analysis in the tourism sector and supports the tourism industry's efforts to secure government support and subsidy (see Higgins-Desbiolles, 2006, pp. 1195-1196). As the UNWTO claims:

Accurately measuring the impact of tourism on national economies can give the industry greater influence with government and the prestige it deserves. That is why the WTO-OMT [UNWTO] has been working with an international group of statistical experts to develop global standards for reporting tourism economic data (UNWTO, no date c).

The UNWTO has long advocated the use of tourism satellite accounts (TSAs) to accurately measure the full size and import of the tourism sector (TSAs are discussed more fully below). Its effort paid off in 2000 when the UN approved the TSA methodology which according to the UNWTO made "tourism the world's first sector to have international standards for measuring its economic impacts in a credible way" (UNWTO, no date a). Pleumarom has criticised the UNWTO's and WTTC's success in getting the TSA accounting system accepted, claiming critics say it is "a statistical exercise mainly aimed to improve the image and stature of the industry and to conceal the considerable economic losses tourist destination countries are experiencing in the face of worldwide growing volatility and progressive liberalization policies" (Pleumarom, no date b).

Because membership of the UNWTO is dominated by developing countries, this organisation wields strong rhetoric on the contributions tourism can make to development. The UNWTO liaises with other international bodies focused on development, including the United Nations Convention on Trade and Development (UNCTAD) and the UNDP. One of the primary functions of the UNWTO's various regional wings is to "... act as a liaison between tourism authorities and the United Nations Development Programme to create specific

---

[48] On the website, there are five headings on UNWTO's programmes: Education; Market intelligence and promotion; Quality and trade in tourism; Statistics and economic measurement of tourism and Sustainable development of tourism (see http://www.world-tourism.org).

development projects" (UNWTO, no date a). The UNWTO also views the transfer of tourism know-how to developing countries to be one of its "fundamental tasks". It is charged with the duty of providing assistance to members in securing finance, obtaining experts and carrying out tourism development plans for new or existing tourism destinations. It is involved in long-term, strategic planning such as developing a tourism master plan for Pakistan in 2001, development of national parks in Rwanda in 1999 and an integrated development plan for the Palestinian Authority in 2000 (UNWTO, no date a). It has also undertaken short-term specific projects such as assisting Syria with tourism legislation and developing an ecotourism plan for Lithuania (UNWTO, no date a). In general though, it could be said that the UNWTO serves the purpose of encouraging developing countries to open up to tourism as they pursue economic development. Pleumarom (no date b) argues that the tourism industry members of the UNWTO form part of the system of "corporate rule in tourism" along with the WTTC, the tourism TNCs in the World Economic Forum and associated supranational governance bodies such as the OECD, the IMF and the World Bank. All are committed to promoting liberalisation in the tourism sector as being good for developing countries while simultaneously serving their own corporate interests.

What is perhaps most unique and eye-catching about the UNWTO is the close relationship that this international organisation has with industry. "WTO is the only inter-governmental organization that offers membership to the operating sector and in this way offers a unique contact point for discussion between government officials and industry leaders" (UNWTO, no date a). While the UNWTO currently has 145 state members and seven territories that hold associate membership there are additionally numerous affiliate members from airlines, hotel chains, tourism operators, consulting firms, tourism professional associations, tourism boards and educational institutions.[49] What is strikingly missing from this list of affiliate members are non-government organisations, particularly those that are critical of tourism, perhaps because the yearly membership fee is $US1700 (Hall, 2000, p. 110). Advocating against the corporate rule of tourism, Pleumarom has called on activists concerned about tourism to join the new movements challenging capitalist globalisation and oppose a UNWTO hitched to the corporate agenda (Pleumarom, no date b). She has stated that the accession of the UNWTO to status as a specialised agency of the UN provides an opportunity to force the UNWTO to adhere to the human rights, developmentalist and interdependency agendas of the wider UN body, particularly should a "citizens charter" be negotiated in the near future (Pleumarom, no date b). However current

---

[49] See http://www.world-tourism.org/frameset/frame_affiliate_directory.html

membership and voting patterns see the UNWTO emerge as a strange hybrid, where its acts officially as an intergovernmental international organisation (as only member states and territories vote); whereas the affiliate members from the tourism business sector wield tremendous weight and influence, particularly through the Business Council.[50]

The UNWTO's Business Council (WTOBC) is very significant when examining the UNWTO's institutional role in supporting capitalist globalisation. It is important to reiterate that of all the UN's specialised agencies and affiliated organisations as well as other international organisations, the UNWTO is unique in having its membership open to the "operating sector" (UNWTO, no date a). It is in the Business Council that the tourism operating sector is most influential, as "airlines, hotel chains, tour operators, trade associations, consultants, promotion boards and educational institutions make up approximately 350 members of the UNWTO Business Council" (UNWTO, no date a). The WTOBC views its mission as "representing and fostering the views of business stakeholders in tourism" (WTOBC, no date). Two of the objectives that support this mission include:

- Ensure private / public sector dialogue and cooperation, both inside and outside WTO [UNWTO] and ensure private sector participation in WTO [UNWTO]… meetings and seminars.
- Assist WTO [UNWTO] in creating the global framework within which the tourism industry operates efficiently, by representing private sector views within that policy dialogue (WTOBC, no date).

The WTOBC is the section of the UNWTO that holds the representatives of the transnational capitalist class (TCC) and expresses the views of the transnational corporations (TNCs). While the WTOBC, like the rest of the UNWTO, expresses a commitment to sustainability and poverty alleviation, what emerges from its activities is full support for the liberalisation agenda of capitalist globalisation. This includes granting an increased voice and representational power for the private sector in the institutions of governance, as well as forceful pushing of TNC agendas such as the General Agreement on Trade in Services discussed below. Pleumarom notes that UNWTO documents have described the

---

[50] Interestingly, at a Tourism Policy Forum convened by the UNWTO in 2004, the Washington Declaration on Tourism as a Sustainable Development Strategy was pronounced. This made a commitment "to recognize the uniqueness of the business perspective as different from that of the public sector and to communicate effectively in business language" (UNWTO & George Washington University, 2004).

WTOBC as "more active and vocal" in the UNWTO's meetings and programmes and she suggests that this is evidence of "corporate power in tourism" being visibly exercised (Pleumarom, no date b). While the UNWTO may claim to be supporting the development agendas of its membership base, a majority of whom are developing countries, the influential role of the WTOBC sees the UNWTO act as an international lobbying body for the powerful tourism TNCs in contradiction to its obligations to a majority of its members.

This disjunction between mandate and effective implementation is also apparent in other spheres. The UNWTO has made a strong commitment to environmental sustainability. On its website, the environment section claims:

> Its message of encouraging low-impact sustainable tourism development rather than uncontrolled mass tourism has been embraced in recent years by WTO [UNWTO] members. They understand that government, in partnership with the private sector, have a responsibility to keep the environment in good condition for future generations and for the future success of the tourism sector (UNWTO, no date c).

As part of this effort, the UNWTO has participated in such major events as the 1992 Rio Summit on Sustainable Development and the Environment and "...former WTO [UNWTO] Secretary-General Antonio Enriquez Savignac ... was instrumental in getting tourism included in Agenda 21 as one of the only industries capable of providing an economic incentive for preservation of the environment" (UNWTO, no date c). However, how genuine this commitment is to sustainability when the agenda of the UNWTO, like its industry members, is focused on continual growth in tourism, remains open to question. The Secretary General of the UNWTO stated at the ITB Berlin Travel Fair in 1996:

> With very, very few exceptions, we are paying only lip service to the ideals of protecting the environment through sustainable tourism. At the same time, we are repeating the same mistakes of the past by going after big numbers, regardless of their impact on the environment or social structures.
> Our fragile planet cannot take it and our increasingly sophisticated travellers will not stand for it. How much longer will it be before a new generation of travellers decides to stay at home rather than deal with a crowded resort? (Antonio Savignac cited in Elliot, 1997, p. 263).

Despite this observation from one of its leaders, the UNWTO actively promotes growth in the tourism sector. While the UNWTO is primarily financed by the membership fees it charges, it is increasingly driven to seek other sources of revenue such as consultancies and is pushed to further cooperation with industry which Hall suggests may affect the "focus of WTO [UNWTO] organisational policies" (2000, p. 110). In fact, one of the main interests of industry which the UNWTO supports is growth. According to Burns "it is clear…that the WTO [UNWTO] is actively promoting the expansion of tourism at a global level. WTO [UNWTO] survives not so much through its membership fees but through spin-off activities such as consulting and project management. It therefore actually needs more tourism!" (cited in Hall, 2000, p. 112). One can easily identify this support for the continued expansion of tourism from the "tourism enriches campaign" which is a public marketing initiative of the UNWTO to promote tourism growth by fostering "communication about the benefits of tourism as the most prospective economic activity for the local communities and countries" (UNWTO, 2004). Such an agenda demonstrates the dynamics of the "growth fetish" which underpins capitalist globalisation (Hamilton, 2003) under the guise of promoting economic growth for the host countries.

An assessment of the power and influence of the UNWTO must also acknowledge important countries in the global community that have not yet joined, including the USA and the UK. When Hall wrote his book on tourism planning, the USA, UK, Canada and Australia were non-members of the UNWTO and Hall surmised that lack of interest in subscribing might be due to both an assumed lack of benefits from membership and perhaps an inability to "influence the direction of WTO [UNWTO] policies and undertakings as they might wish" (2000, p. 110) since developing countries represent a majority of members. However, alternatively, it might have demonstrated these governments' lack of insight into the importance of supranational action in the tourism arena or alternatively that the important activities that secure the interest of their large TNCs are occurring elsewhere, such as in the negotiations of the General Agreement on Trade in Services (GATS) and WTTC. The fact that Canada and Australia recently joined might indicate that the stature and importance of the UNWTO (and perhaps tourism itself) are on the rise. It could be anticipated that the UNWTO's full integration with the UN would enhance such an effect.

3.3.2. The World Travel and Tourism Council

The World Travel and Tourism Council (WTTC) is another important institution of international tourism. The WTTC describes itself in this way:

> The World Travel and Tourism Council is a Global Business Leaders' Forum for Travel and Tourism. Its Members are Chief Executives from all sectors of [the Tourism] Industry... Its central goal is to work with governments to realise the full potential economic impact of the world's largest generator of wealth and jobs - Travel and Tourism (WTTC, no date b).

Its members include some of the most powerful TNCs in the tourism industry including British Airways, American Express, the Thomas Cook Group, Touristik Union International (better known as TUI A. G.), the SABRE Group and Hilton Hotels Corporation. To achieve its goal of promoting travel and tourism growth to the world's governments, it pushes for the removal of barriers to the growth of the tourism industry. As an unabashed advocate of tourism growth, it can be seen as complicit in the rapid expansion of global tourism destinations and a contributor to the growth fetish evident in tourism.

The WTTC currently has several initiatives underway which provide an insight into its role in capitalist globalisation. Perhaps most prominent is the *Blueprint for new tourism*, initiated in 2003. It is here we find the WTTC emphasising and perhaps exaggerating the importance of the tourism industry in order to garner greater government support. Two features predominate in this document: an emphasis on growth and a call for governments to take tourism more seriously. It sets three agendas which include government recognition of travel and tourism as a "top priority"; the need for business to balance "economics with people, culture and environment"; and all parties to share "the pursuit of long-term growth and prosperity" (WTTC, 2003). Under each of these areas, the WTTC sets out a list of responsibilities for governments and industry to bring about this "new tourism". These include:

1. Governments must recognize travel and tourism as a top priority.

To meet this first condition, governments must:

- Elevate travel and tourism as an issue to the top level of policy making
- Create a competitive business environment
- Ensure that quality statistics and data feed into policy and decision-making
- Invest in developing the appropriate human capital
- Liberalise trade, transport, communications and investment
- Build confidence in safety and security
- Promote product diversification that spreads demand

- Plan for sustainable tourism growth, in keeping with cultures and character
- Invest in new technology, such as satellite navigation systems

2. Business must balance economics with people, culture and environment

To meet the second condition, the industry must:

- Expand markets while protecting natural resources, local heritage and lifestyles
- Develop people to narrow the gap between the 'haves' and 'have-nots'
- Provide traditional tourism products sensitively
- Reduce seasonality and increase yields with imaginative new products
- Improve quality, value and choice
- Agree and implement quality standards at all levels
- Transfer skills and best practice throughout the industry
- Increase the sophistication of information, to make better business decisions
- Communicate more broadly and more effectively

3. All parties must share the pursuit of long-term growth and prosperity

To meet the third condition, all the main stakeholders must:

- Ally best practice in tourism with government policy
- Prepare sustainable master plans for entire destinations
- Create locally driven processes for continuous stakeholder consultation
- Restructure national tourism boards
- Set environmental policy goals that can be met
- Develop and deploy skills effectively
- Collaborate on information requirements
- Collaborate on security
- Develop confidence on all sides (WTTC, 2003).

An evaluation of these lists clearly indicates the growth agenda of the WTTC and even though one of the key agendas is for business to "balance economics with the interests of people, culture and environment", only two items under this heading are not related to fostering more growth, that is "develop people to narrow the gap between the 'haves' and 'have-nots'" and "transfer skills and best practice throughout the industry". Under the lead injunction that "governments must recognize travel and tourism as a top priority" one can clearly see the capitalist globalisation agenda as even the discussion of sustainability is phrased in terms of "sustainable tourism *growth*". What is really disturbing about the *Blueprint for new tourism* when read with a critical eye to uncover the dynamics of capitalist globalisation, is the appropriation of alternative tourism terminology by the WTTC. Adopting the language of "new tourism", the WTTC evokes an image of a sensitive and more sustainable tourism, when what is evident in the detail is an agenda for accelerating growth and profit to the tourism TNCs that make up the WTTC.

Another main activity of the WTTC is promotion of research into the tourism satellite account (TSA). TSA is a method of estimating the size of the tourism industry which has been promoted by the UNWTO and the WTTC. Tourism requires a special accounting system in order to address the fact that it is a complex phenomenon that overlaps with other economic sectors and is not defined by its product but rather by the consumer of its goods and services. The WTTC's TSA includes personal travel and tourism expenditure by an economy's residents, the export income that comes from international visitor spending in the local economy, business travel, government expenditure (on such things as cultural museums, national parks, aviation administration and marketing campaigns), capital investment and exports of consumer or capital goods to tourism and travel providers (i.e. cruise ships, airplanes, food, etc.). The WTTC states:

> Travel and tourism is an industrial activity defined by the diverse collection of products (durables and non-durables) and services (transportation, accommodation, food and beverage, entertainment, government services, etc.) that are delivered to visitors. There are two basic aggregates of demand (Travel and Tourism Consumption and Total Demand) and by employing input/output modelling separately to these two aggregates the Satellite Account is able to produce two different and complementary aggregates of Travel and Tourism Supply; the Travel and Tourism Industry and the Travel and Tourism Economy. The former captures the explicitly defined production-side 'industry' contribution (i.e. direct impact only), for comparison with all other industries, while the latter captures the broader 'economy-wide' impact, direct and indirect, of Travel and Tourism (WTTC, 2005b, p. 11).

Focus on the TSA allows the compilation of statistics and predictions. Thus tourism's global contribution for 2006 was predicted to provide:

- US$ 6,477.2 billion of economic activity,
- 10.3% of total GDP,
- 234,305,000 jobs, or 8.7% of total employment (WTTC, no date a).

The WTTC has overseen the development of TSAs for numerous economies in the global community in order to underscore the economic impact of tourism and improve the lobbying potential of tourism industry supporters that comprise its membership. What is difficult to reconcile is the positive rhetoric of official documents with the negative outcomes as manifest in economic leakages and costs exposed in several studies such as Brohman (1996), Duffy (2002), Patullo (1996) and Pleumarom (1999a). Because the WTTC is interested in the global trading practices of tourism, represents big tourism TNCs and is in effect a global corporate lobby group, the TSAs are selected as a tool to serve the corporate interest in promoting the tourism sector and gaining governmental support to expand tourism. They do not however tell the (failed) developmental story of leakages nor the negative human impacts of tourism that concern such analysts as Brohman (1996) and critics such as Pleumarom (1999a).

In addition to these initiatives, the WTTC has also undertaken a "competitiveness monitor" which "tracks a wide range of information, which indicates to what extent a country offers a competitive environment for Travel and Tourism development" (WTTC, no date a). The WTTC describes its purpose as aiming "to stimulate policy-makers, industry investors, academics and all other interested parties to recognize the crucial role they play in maximizing the contribution of Travel and Tourism for the benefit of everyone and to ensure that the development of the industry is sustainable" (WTTC, no date a). This monitor is therefore perhaps more logically seen as a tool the WTTC provides for TNCs to plan their most profitable and successful investments in a range of countries lured by the promise of tourism.

Additionally, the WTTC has a corporate social leadership initiative. It is in this domain that the WTTC claims a long affiliation with the sustainability movement and boasts of its support for applying Agenda 21 to the travel and tourism sector, its latest support for the poverty alleviation agenda of tourism, its creation of the Tourism for Tomorrow Awards and its alliances with groups such as Green Globe, CyberDodo and the Sustainable Tourism Cooperative Research Centre in Australia (WTTC, no date a). The WTTC can be challenged on whether its commitment to corporate social responsibility (CSR) represents a change in business practice or whether it is merely geared to good public relations. The WTTC publication *Corporate social leadership in travel and tourism* (WTTC, 2002) provides useful material for analysis. This document features a focus on the business case for commitment to CSR agendas. It emphasises the "new consumer", or tourists with a conscience, who are increasingly discerning of corporate business practice who therefore present a lucrative business opportunity.[51] More significantly, the content of some of the case studies which are presented as exemplars of corporate leadership represent little advance on ordinary corporate charity and do not indicate a rethinking of corporate social roles (see for instance the cases of Radisson SAS Hotels and Resorts, TUI A. G. and Uniglobe) (WTTC, 2002).

It is also telling that this report states categorically that "a voluntary approach is crucial… attempting to regulate social responsibility would not only be impractical, given the diverse needs of different communities, it would undermine the personal commitment and creativity that fuel it" (WTTC, 2002, p. 5). Such voluntary approaches amount to corporate self-regulation. Naomi Klein argues that corporate self-regulation gives "unprecedented power [to corporations]…the power to draft their own privatised legal systems, to investigate and police themselves, as quasi nation-states" (2001, p. 437). In terms of tourism, Mowforth and Munt argue that corporate social responsibility and codes of conduct can be seen as "exercises in public relations" and attempts to court the ethical consumer (2003, p. 194); they can also be seen as attempts to pre-empt government regulation of tourism activities. Thus we can see that the WTTC effectively restricts the movement for corporate responsibility to the confines of TNC control while sustaining the corporate interest.

Along these same lines, the WTTC was the initiator of the Green Globe program that was created to implement the principles applicable to the travel and tourism industry under Agenda 21 from the 1992 Earth Summit at Rio. It provides information on environmental improvement projects, achievement awards, and a certification process to achieve Green Globe status which is wholly voluntary (Green Globe, no date). The Green Globe project has nevertheless had its critics: in the Green Travel internet discussion forum, some have seen the Green Globe awards merely as "greenwash"; others have noted that it has evolved positively by separating from the WTTC and promoting environmental sustainability in a pragmatic manner and that it therefore needs and deserves the support of "responsible operators'" to succeed (Green Travel, 1999). In their political analysis of tourism, Mowforth and Munt argue that Green Globe is an example of the WTTC and the UNWTO advocating self-regulation in order to secure their

---

[51] This phenomenon is analysed both in the report and also prominently addressed in the first appendix of the publication.

members' interests and avoid outside regulation (2003, pp. 184-185). They conclude:

> Self-regulation led by bodies such as the WTTC and the WTO/OMT [UNWTO], whose stated aims are the promotion of the tourism industry rather than its restraint, is likely to lead to policies which further the pursuit of profits in a business world where profit maximisation and capital accumulation is the logic of economic organisation (Mowforth and Munt, 2003, p. 185).

Thus similar to the way in which the World Economic Forum, the IMF and the WTO support transnational practices and the interests of the transnational capitalist class that underpin capitalist globalisation (Sklair, 2002), there is evidence that the UNWTO and the WTTC support a corporate tourism agenda that is symbiotic with capitalist globalisation.

3.3.3. The World Bank and World Economic Forum: Non-Tourism Institutions Foster the Corporate Tourism Agenda

For a decade, between 1969 and 1979, the World Bank Group maintained a special department focused on tourism in recognition of the rapid growth of tourism and its importance to the foreign exchange earnings of many of the Bank's member countries (Davis and Simmons, 1982, p. 212). While the World Bank disbanded this tourism section over 20 years ago when it abandoned its support of direct tourism development projects after receiving much criticism (Richter, 1989), it has remained very active in the promotion of tourism for development. In 1998, it co-hosted with the UNWTO a conference entitled "Tourism Visions for the 21st Century" to raise the profile of tourism in development planning. Whether the tourism projects supported by the World Bank in recent years are more successful than those devised by its tourism department in the past is subject to debate; however what is clear is that such support goes to develop infrastructure and tie an economy into the international tourism economy, and in many cases adds to a developing country's debt burden.[52]

---

[52] For instance in 2005, Madagascar was given a "credit" of nearly US$130 million to develop tourism in a growth-pole strategy in two underdeveloped regions, Nosy Be and Taolagnaro (World Bank, 2005).

Ideologically, therefore the World Bank's intervention in tourism can be seen to be part of the capitalist globalisation process described by Sklair (2002) and a component of the "market fundamentalism" described by Gill (1995). A representative of the UNWTO in an interview stated "we have some of the same goals as the international finance community ... tourism is a great way of generating foreign currency, improving a country's roads and public works, and creating jobs in rural areas, where tourists like to go" (World Bank News, 1998). Taken at face value, this statement seems innocent enough, but when making the connections between "the neo-liberal market civilisation" that Gill describes and the tourism structure which contributes to it, the statement of coincidental interest of the UNWTO and the international finance community is more concerning; it is referring to the radical shift of economies to full integration into global markets. World Bank-sponsored tourism projects have also come in for criticism because their investments are less geared to developmental outcomes for locals than serving the interests of powerful entities in the corporate sector, governments and/or rich-world tourists. As Mowforth and Munt have remarked international financial institutions (IFIs) such as the World Bank have power over any country that requires financial assistance and under the market system, tourism is treated "much the same as any other cash crop" (2003, p. 261). There are numerous examples that illustrate the impacts of such developments. For instance, a World Bank sponsored ecotourism program (co-sponsored by a Japanese aid agency) in Thailand has seen illegal and inappropriate developments in protected areas (supported by the Tourism Authority of Thailand) catering to the Thai elite and wealthy international tourists despite the protest of locals and laws prohibiting such developments (Tourism Investigation and Monitoring Team, no date a). Similarly, Mowforth and Munt discuss the case of Grenada in the Caribbean, which prior to US destabilisation and invasion in the early 1980s, was set to implement a socialist-inspired tourism program (2003, pp. 259-260). After the US intervention, Grenada became a model of corporatised tourism as the US development agency, United States Agency for International Development (USAID), intervened to establish tourism infrastructures and developments attractive to TNC investors but with poor developmental outcomes for the populace (Mowforth and Munt, 2003, pp. 259-260).

It is also important to note that the travel and tourism sectors have received some attention from the World Economic Forum (WEF), a non-government organisation that is made up of "the world's 1,000 leading companies, along with 200 smaller businesses" including global giants such as Unilever, Pfizer and Nestle (WEF, no date). The WEF is the target of virulent opposition from the "anti-globalisation" movement because it is seen as a vital agent of antidemocratic capitalist globalisation and as a facilitator of the interest of the TCC. A look at the WEF's website indicates its support for corporate-led globalisation and corporatised tourism.[53] For instance, the WEF held a forum on liberalisation in the civil aviation sector in 2004 in Jordan at which the tourism industry agenda was effectively promoted by various speakers. Geoffrey Lipman, a special adviser to the Secretary-General of the UNWTO, advocated the growth of aviation and tourism suggesting they can be catalysts for peace. Thomas R. Pickering, representing Boeing, predicted the Middle Eastern region was ripe for tourism growth (and therefore presumably "ripe for" for buying Boeing's planes) (WEF, 2004). In fact, one WTTC document claimed that in 2005, "WTTC and the WEF continued to support each other in their respective ventures this year" (WTTC, 2005a, p. 27). This simple statement suggests how global tourism institutions interact and reinforce the institutions fostering capitalist globalisation and the marketisation agenda. In other contexts, we have already seen that such trends do not prioritise grassroots development or an equitable share of proceeds from tourism.

2.4. TRANSNATIONAL CAPITALIST CLASS - A CASE STUDY

Sklair's analysis of capitalist globalisation suggests that critical analysis of TNCs is insufficient to understand the effects of capitalist globalisation as the roles of the TCC are also very significant (2002). One prime example of a member of the TCC who operates in the sphere of corporate tourism is Geoffrey Lipman who has wielded great power and influence.[54] Lipman has held numerous posts of influence within the travel and tourism sector including serving as president of the WTTC and executive director of the International Air Transport Association. He is currently serving as a special adviser to the Secretary-General of the UNWTO, has been a prominent advocate of liberalisation in the aviation sector and has taken part in WEF events concerned with tourism.[55] Lipman has also chaired Green Globe 21 (applying Agenda 21 standards to the tourism sector) and currently promotes the International Council of Tourism Partners whose focus is on alleviating poverty through tourism. Such initiatives can be interpreted as public relations efforts to head off the criticism that tourism and globalisation receive due to their role in fostering ecological and sociological crises (as

---

[53] http://www.weforum.org/site/knowledgenavigator.nsf/Content/Travel+and+Tourism
[54] Lipman is an example of a member of both the state and technical fractions of the TCC during his varied career (see Sklair's typology, 2002, p. 99).
[55] See: http://www.weforum.org/site/knowledgenavigator.nsf/Content/Lipman%20Geoffrey

described by Sklair, 2002). Whether TCC leaders such as Lipman are sincere in their roles is not the point; they probably are in some cases. What is the point is how their efforts in forums such as the UNWTO and WEF serve the interests of the corporate class (TCC) and advance the success of capitalist globalisation. For instance, Pleumarom (1999b, p. 5) has noted how Lipman, when serving as President of the WTTC, visited Thailand to campaign for privatisation of state-owned enterprises. At the same time, WTTC members British Airways and the British Airport Authority made investment bids for Thai Airways and Thai airports which were seen as a corporate assault on the Thai travel and transport sector (Pleumarom, 1999b). Tourism consultants like Lipman epitomise the role of TCC "globalising professionals" as they promote and foster the interests of corporate tourism in various forums such as the WEF and the GATS negotiations as well as to governments around the world.

Sklair's typology of the TCC also applies to groups engaged in tourism. For instance, a study of the activities of various fractions of the TCC operating in the travel and tourism sector could shed light on how they promote transnational practices and foster the advance of capitalist globalisation. As hotel, resorts and restaurants sign up to franchising agreements, a study could be made of how global corporate leaders from the headquarters interrelate and cooperate with local affiliates and how such interactions support the agendas of capitalist globalisation. Additionally, the role of the state fraction of the tourism TCC is exposed in reports of the Tourism Investigation and Monitoring Team (TIM-Team) on how the Tourism Authority of Thailand has collaborated in using World Bank social investment money for inappropriate and wholesale tourism development in national parks in violation of Thai laws (TIM-Team, no date a).

Merchants and media (called the "consumerist fraction" of the TCC by Sklair, 2002) also play a vital role in fostering the culture-ideology of consumerism as people have to be urged to contribute to the continual growth demanded by capitalist globalisation and corporatised tourism. This in turn underpins the ability of the TNCs and the TCC to achieve ever higher profits. Such roles are fulfilled by travel publishers such as Lonely Planet Books,[56] the producers of travel magazines such as Conde Nast Travel, as well as individual media personalities such as travel reporter Susan Kurosawa in Australia and television presenter Michael Palin who publicise global travel opportunities to entice tourists.

Additionally a study could be made of the roles of entrepreneurs such as Richard Branson of Virgin and "Screw" Turner of Flight Centre to show how

---

[56] For example Tony Wheeler, publisher of Lonely Planet, advocated travel to Burma when human rights organisations and other travel businesses were calling for a boycott.

their approaches add more than flamboyance and brashness to the tourism industry. They have in fact created global corporate empires built on fostering the consumerism of youth. This chapter cannot detail such cases because of its primary concern to maintain a macro-level analysis of global structures and dynamics. We thus return to some of the examples of transnational practices operating in the corporate tourism sector to see how the dynamics of capitalist globalisation are evident here.

3.5. TOURISM TRANSNATIONAL PRACTICES

3.5.1. Liberalisation under the General Agreement on Trade and Services (GATS)

For decades, the transnational capitalist class and other supporters of capitalist globalisation have been pushing a free trade agenda and open access to the world's wealth and resources through multilateral trade talks such as the Uruguay Round and since 1995, through the institutional structure of the World Trade Organization (WTO). More recently, attention has focused on the services sector, including tourism, through the promotion of the General Agreement on Trade in Services (GATS). As the NGO Equations[57] has suggested, the highest rates of growth in tourism are being achieved in developing countries as "new tourists" are drawn to their natural and cultural attractions. As a result, the big TNCs are keen to liberalise the tourism sector so that they can pursue the profit opportunities arising in the developing world (Equations, 2001).

The impacts of the liberalisation of tourism services must be seen within the context of the wider liberalisation process. As tourism is being subjected to liberalisation, so are the sectors with which tourism interrelates including agriculture, financial services, investment, construction, communications, transport and aviation. This establishes a system of "interlocking liberalization" which Williams claims can "create dependency on the market, with impacts on food security…[which] may prove negative for social development" (M. Williams, 2002, p. 12). This "interlocking liberalization" includes a series of agreements that create a structure which is conducive to corporate interests,[58] including the multilateral negotiations of the WTO, the Agreement on Trade-

---

[57] Equations in a tourism NGO based in Bangalore, India.
[58] Mowforth and Munt (2003, p. 266) cite a European Community document of 2000 which describes GATS as "first and foremost an instrument for the benefit of business".

Related Investment Measures (TRIMS), Trade-Related Aspects of Intellectual Property Rights Agreement (TRIPS) and the one under discussion here, GATS. These agreements are augmented by numerous regional and bilateral agreements such as the North America Free Trade Agreement (NAFTA). While all of these measures are the result of extensive negotiations to create a "consensus"-based structure of rules on the conduct of global free trade, critics argue that the less powerful countries are forced into agreements that damage their interests and serve the interests of powerful TNCs and the TCC.[59]

But it is GATS which is most effective within the tourism domain. At the same time that multilateral negotiations on trade in goods and agricultural produce were being negotiated at the Uruguay round and the WTO in the 1990s, attention was turned to the growing sector of trade in services. This led to the creation of the GATS in 1994 and its continued development through subsequent negotiations has been overseen by the WTO. The most recent negotiations are occurring in the Doha round of talks which began in 2001 and have specifically focused on services. The GATS rests on three key concepts, including most favoured nation treatment, market access and national treatment. The most favoured nation treatment clause commits members to treat services and service suppliers of any other member no less favourably than they treat services and service suppliers of any other country. The market access provision requires members to allow market access to foreign investors in the sectors which they have identified under GATS. The GATS' national treatment clause requires members to treat foreign corporations in the same way they treat domestic companies operating in the specified service sectors under the agreement's provisions. Additionally GATS has a clause on "general exceptions" concerning the right for members to apply general exceptions to their commitments on "public morals and human, animal or plant life or health" (Hoad, 2002, p. 217).

GATS deals with "tourism and travel related services" and divides these into four subsectors including:

---

[59] For instance, Mowforth and Munt quote the NGO the World Development Movement (WDM) who claim that great pressure is exerted by the developed countries on the developing countries in these negotiations including the inference that if the developing county negotiators do not act as advised, then aid might be affected (WDM cited in Mowforth & Munt, 2003, p. 266). Williams also notes that liberalisation in the tourism sector of developing countries needs to be understood within the context of structural adjustment imposed by the IFIs (M. Williams, 2002, p. 12). Lastly, Hoad notes that GATS has an expansionary character as member countries are continually pressed to return to negotiations for further commitments: Hoad claims GATS "is the only trade agreement that mandates WTO members ... return to the negotiating table on a regular basis" (2002, p. 224).

- hotels and restaurants,
- travel agencies and tour operators,
- tourist guide services,
- and an "other" category (unspecified).

The GATS liberalisation program was proceeding in ongoing talks of the Doha round under the auspices of the WTO and a target had been set to achieve some locked-in commitments under the agreement by the end of 2005. Proponents of liberalisation like the UNWTO argue that countries of both the developed and developing world will benefit from the liberalisation under the GATS. The former expect greater business opportunities for their corporations and the latter are promised more opportunities for development through the "North-South flows" (UNWTO, 2003b). Such a "win-win" perspective seems illusory, however, since these talks recently collapsed in part because developing countries remain unconvinced of such promises.[60] The following discussion will highlight some of the difficulties GATS presents for developing countries.

Despite the alleged convergence of interests, there is a clear distinction between the bargaining positions of developed countries such as the United States and the member states of the European Union and the positions of developing countries. In 2000 for example, the United States requested the removal of several barriers or protections that impeded its businesses including such practices as limiting the repatriation of profits, requiring the employment of locals, providing domestic businesses with subsidies and support, restricting the sale or rent of property and restricting the share of foreign investment in joint ventures, all of which assisted developing countries to create a viable tourism sector and ensured that the local economy obtained significant benefits from it (Berne Declaration and Working Group on Tourism and Development, 2004, p. 10). According to Menotti (2002), the European Union likewise made a specific approach to Mexico under the GATS to ask it to lift its requirement that developers of hotels and restaurants hold a permit. This provision was imposed by Mexico as a part of its planning process to promote sustainable tourism practices in its growing tourism sector. In contrast Thailand has expressed support for the liberalisation under

---

[60] In July, 2006, Muqbil reported "the collapse of the World Trade Organization talks in Geneva last week is a major victory for developing countries, as well as the civil society non-governmental organisations which have long been urging them to resist pressure to sign lop-sided deals that may generate short-term gain but ultimately result in long-term pain. The time-out has given developing countries some breathing room to reassess the state of play before deciding if and how to go forward. International relations today are not characterised by level playing fields. Now, governments have clearly indicated a desire to say 'enough is enough' to double standards" (2006).

GATS but voiced concerns over the ability of developing countries to ensure environmental and cultural protection when opening up to the global economy (Noypayak, 2001). Additionally delegations from Central American countries have raised major concerns during the GATS discussion about the anti-competitive practices by tourism TNCs (Communication from the Dominican Republic, El Salvador and Honduras, 2000).[61] UNCTAD has identified the main concerns of developing countries that are relevant under GATS:

- the fact that the small to medium enterprises (SMEs) characteristic of the tourism sector in developing countries are likely to be overrun by the TNCs that will take advantage of liberalisation's effects to invest in these economies undergoing considerable tourism growth rates,
- developing countries require a multilateral 'open skies' policy where current charter restrictions, flight density restrictions and high pricing policies could be dealt with and where they can fairly access the computer reservations systems currently controlled by the TNCs of the North,
- developing countries also have issues of access to the facilities of electronic commerce as the global distribution systems are controlled by the major carriers who privilege the major tourism service providers over the SMEs characteritic of developing countries (cited in M. Williams, 2002, pp. 14-15).

Additionally, whereas developing countries would most benefit from the free movement of personnel, the restrictive immigration policies of the developed world make it unlikely that tourism employees of the developing world will find tourism jobs as easy to access in the developed world as developed world tourism workers have found it in the developing countries. Movement of people is under mode four[62] of the agreement and developing countries have been keen to see

---

[61] UNCTAD has described these anti-competitive practices quite precisely: "The liberalisation and globalisation of the travel and tourism sectors have also led to a high concentration of a few international firms in key sectors, including organized travel, international booking, marketing and sales of tourism and related activities. The high concentration in these sectors creates market power and the potential for the abuse of dominance by large international firms. This often translates into exclusionary agreements, price fixing, market sharing among dominant operators or boycott and refusal to deal with operators in developing countries. These anti-competitive agreements and conduct impose enormous costs and eliminate benefits, which developing countries may reap from the liberalisation and expansion of world tourism" (UNCTAD, no date).

[62] The GATS distinguishes between four modes of supplying services: cross-border trade, consumption abroad, commercial presence, and presence of natural persons.

access of people from developing countries to short term opportunities in developed countries without such access being tied to commercial presence.[63] The requirement of linking access to commercial presence works to the advantage of the developed countries that have rich TNCs that can establish a commercial presence in developing countries (Khor, 2003).[64]

In sum, because the tourism sector in many developing countries is characterised by SMEs, the only advantages that a liberalisation regime could offer these countries is real technical assistance and technology transfer of such things as computer reservation systems; requisite protection of their domestic sectors until such time as they are able to compete; and movement of tourism personnel to where the jobs are available. A reflection of the seriousness of these diverging concerns is the WTO's efforts to convene symposia and discussions such as the Symposium on Tourism Services held in February, 2001 to address the concerns of developing countries over GATS negotiations (WTO, 2001). It appears that the promoters of the liberalisation agenda fear a failure to forge ahead on fronts such as GATS in a climate of anti-globalisation endangers the entire project. Nonetheless, developing countries have so far resisted having an unfair GATS agreement imposed upon them (Khor, 2005; Muqbil, 2006).

Another important point of difference between the developed and developing countries arose during the negotiations for the GATS. Originally GATS was meant to proceed in liberalisation in a "positive list" approach whereby each member country made commitments in each of the sectors that it felt prepared to

---

- Cross-border supply is defined to cover services flows from the territory of one Member into the territory of another Member (e.g. banking or architectural services transmitted via telecommunications or mail);
- Consumption abroad refers to situations where a service consumer (e.g. tourist or patient) moves into another Member's territory to obtain a service;
- Commercial presence implies that a service supplier of one Member establishes a territorial presence, including through ownership or lease of premises, in another Member's territory to provide a service (e.g. domestic subsidiaries of foreign insurance companies or hotel chains); and
- Presence of natural persons consists of persons of one Member entering the territory of another Member to supply a service (e.g. accountants, doctors or teachers). The Annex on Movement of Natural Persons specifies, however, that Members remain free to operate measures regarding citizenship, residence or access to the employment market on a permanent basis (WTO, no date).

[63] Studies by Alan Winters have shown that "increasing developed countries' quotas for mode 4 by 3 percent of their labour forces would generate annual gains of over US$150 billion" (cited in Khor, 2003).

[64] Khor says that developed countries have "piled on" the pressure on developing countries to commit on mode 3 which allows foreign enterprises to establish commercial presence in a wide range of tourism related sectors while failing to respond to the developing countries' calls to make commitments on liberalising under mode 4 (Khor, 2003).

commit to and placed the limitations to these commitments as that country's interest required.[65] However, following an initiative of the Dominican Republic, El Salvador and Honduras in 1999, some countries began to call for a specific tourism annex to the GATS agreement in which a cluster approach to liberalisation could be undertaken. Under this Annex, the products and services specifically related to tourism will be comprehensively listed so that tourism can obtain clear and comprehensive treatment not provided under the general GATS agreement (Communication from the Dominican Republic, El Salvador, Honduras, Nicaragua and Panama, 2000). While the cluster approach is called a "developing country" initiative, the US, the EU and Australia have come out firmly in favour of it (Equations, 2001) because they oppose the "positive list approach" allowing member countries to approach liberalisation in a piecemeal fashion in order to protect their own national circumstances. They view this as being against their interests since the big investors and corporations they represent benefit from a wholesale liberalisation rather than a gradualist and conservative approach. Developing countries, on the other hand, even those more well advanced such as India and Brazil, benefit more from the "positive list approach" so that they can protect weaker sectors (particularly in the informal economy), gather the required information to engage in liberalisation in an informed manner and develop the necessary policies and regulations to secure sustainability and social welfare (Equations, 2001). Therefore, the positive list proposal is a more satisfactory approach for harnessing tourism for the welfare of developing societies, while the cluster proposal suits the supporters of liberalisation who want to liberalise the tourism market which serves the interests of TNCs and the TCC who stand to benefit from new economic opportunities.

Hoad has provided arguably the best academic analysis to date of the provisions of the GATS and its potential impacts on tourism within the context of sustainability (2002). His analysis of the provisions of the GATS in such areas as market access, most-favoured nation treatment, national treatment and general exceptions reveals some of the real problems with the agreement. For instance, the market access provision is hostile to destination countries attempting to limit the number of service providers through quotas or economic needs testing which is a key component of keeping tourism within the bounds of ecological and sociological carrying capacity. The most-favoured nation treatment and national treatment clauses curtail the ability of governments to favour tourism service

---

[65] Under the current structure of GATS, some tourism and travel related activities can fall under other sectors of commitment, for instance construction (e.g. construction of hotels), business services (such as tourism rental management) and health-related and social services (such as physical fitness facilities) (Hoad, 2002, p. 215).

providers who employ locals or have sound environmental management policies or to reject those who do not. Lastly, Hoad argues that while the general exceptions clause seems to give member countries some ability to limit these commitments on the grounds of social and environmental concerns, past trade disputes reveal that these exceptions would be likely to be judged as discriminatory trade practices and therefore penalised as contravening a country's obligations under GATS (Hoad, 2002, p. 217). Hoad's analysis is a searching investigation of the implications of GATS and reveals why many developing countries and their supporters are concerned with the impacts of its provisions.

GATS has understandably received critical attention from NGOs concerned with the negative impacts of globalisation because of its liberalisation in such vital human welfare service sectors as the provision of water, transport, energy and education. However tourism NGOs such as Equations, Tourism Concern and the TIM-Team have argued that while the tourism sector may appear to be less important than these human welfare sectors, it is arguably no less important (Equations, 2004).[66] The fact that tourism is a service sector of major significance to many countries is perhaps apparent from the fact that more commitments have been made in tourism than in any other service industry under the GATS agreement, with 125 of the WTO's 142 members opening up in at least one of the tourism subsectors (Equations, 2001).

Equations has put together an articulate list of concerns about GATS from a developing country point of view which includes the following: the agreement is geared to the interests of the developed countries; its rules are incomplete and unclear; it will create a loss of local government control through centralising trade policy; it will lead to a "race to the bottom in environmental and developmental standards"; and the GATS has a lock-in effect where countries cannot withdraw from commitments without intolerable costs thus making them irreversible (Equations, 2004).[67]

One of the key concerns is that the trade negotiators liberalising the services sector through the GATS negotiations fail to understand the distinctive complexity and dynamics of the tourism sector. Such distinguishing traits include its overlapping with other sectors such as agriculture, transport, finance and hospitality which means that liberalisation may have complex and unintended

---

[66] Hoad (2002) provides a useful overview of the positions of GATS supporters and GATS opponents.

[67] As a result of the concern with this "locking in" and the penalties that withdrawal could bring, Thailand, Malaysia, Indonesia and the Philippines have led a call for a "safeguard mechanism that can be used to backtrack from GATS commitments when a country's national services enterprises are threatened" (Khor, 2003).

effects. More importantly, tourism is more than just an economic activity, it has attendant sociological and environmental impacts with which the local people must manage to live. Liberalisation in the tourism sector is expected to have widespread impacts on the environment, labour standards and human rights in a multiplicity of locations. These impacts may be particularly adverse in the developing world where policy, management and regulation of the tourism sector may be underdeveloped to deal with such complex outcomes (Pleumarom, no date a). A Swiss NGO, Arbeitskreis Tourismus Entwicklung (AkTE), has stated "These GATS negotiations aim to dismantle basic political frameworks - including environmental legislation and social norms - in favour of economic growth" (Tourism Concern, 2002). Equations has conducted a detailed analysis of the impacts of liberalisation through GATS on the province of Goa, India, where the dynamics of mass tourism have already had major impacts and concludes that GATS will have significant negative outcomes not only for the environment, society and economy of Goa but will also weaken the ability of local governments to govern for the public good (Equations, 2002).[68] One fair trade analyst has described GATS as:

> Designed to ensure that host governments, confronted with powerful transnational corporations who import their own staff and the majority of goods needed for their tourism operation, cannot compel them to use local materials and products to enhance the 'multiplier effect', or to take special measures to secure a competitive base for their domestic businesses (Kalisch, 2001, p.4).

Additionally GATS is predicted to lead to greater concentration in the tourism sector as big tourism TNCs continue the trend in vertical integration which is very evident in places like Germany where the three leading tourism companies control 68 percent of the market (Berne Declaration and WGTD, 2004, pp. 8-9). In developing countries, the dynamics of liberalisation are likely to see SMEs and indigenous enterprises bought out by TNCs seeking investment opportunities in the developing world. Pleumarom describes the likely impacts of liberalisation on the Thai hotel sector as fostering "mergers and acquisitions" (1999b). It should be noted that these impacts are not developmental as they do not create new jobs and economic benefits but instead are likely to increase economic leakages.

Tourism Concern, among other NGOs, has pointed out how the GATS provisions fail to take into account agreements and obligations negotiated in other forums including sustainable tourism, commitments on biodiversity (through the

---

[68] Also see Pleumarom (no date a).

Convention on Biological Diversity), on labour standards (through the International Labour Organization (ILO)), poverty reduction agendas as well as the rights of Indigenous peoples and other minorities (Tourism Concern, 2002).

Hoad's analysis of GATS in 2002 evaluated the impacts of liberalisation on tourism and in particular its effects on tourism sustainability (2002). His critical positioning is evident from his use of sources such as a United Nations Environment Programme (UNEP) report that described increased trade activities promoted by trade liberalisation as having "serious negative environmental and related social impacts" (UNEP cited in Hoad, 2002, p. 220). Hoad's work has provided much needed focus on the impacts of tourism liberalisation under GATS on capacities to secure environmental protection and sustainability. Hoad's analysis (2002) has been followed by the work of Bendell and Font (2004) who read the GATS agreement in a "pro-sustainability" way and argue that environmental protection does not have to be regarded as trade restrictive under the GATS protocols. Lastly, there is the empirical analysis of the impacts of liberalisation on the social and environmental conditions in Turkey undertaken by the Worldwide Fund for Nature (WWF) which found that while it was difficult to ascertain how the Turkish tourism industry fared under liberalisation, there was some evidence of environmental degradation and lack of social benefit (WWF, 2001).

In fact, the effects of liberalisation under GATS should be seen in the broader context of major inequality between the developed and developing world. Many developing countries have been subjected to structural adjustment programmes (SAPs)[69] by IFIs which have put them on the liberalisation juggernaut whether it is in their interest to do so or not. Part of the SAP portfolio in many developing countries has been the promotion of tourism as an avenue to development. Subject to crushing debts, dependent on development assistance and subject to financial crises due to the financial speculation and ease of movement of capital, some developing countries are compelled into forums such as GATS when it might not be in their interest to do so, and they are compelled to make commitments before the implications are clear. Pleumarom exposes how powerful TNCs take advantage of such situations to obtain corporate advantage. Specifically, she discusses the roles of finance giants Goldman Sachs and Merrill Lynch in the conduct of structural adjustment in developing countries and in the liberalisation of the Thai travel and tourism sector (1999b).

---

[69] SAPs have been renamed Poverty Reduction Strategy Papers (PRSPs) (Mowforth & Munt, 2003, p. 28) perhaps as a result of the criticism that anti-globalisation activists have levelled at IFIs such as the IMF and World Bank.

Not unexpectedly, the UNWTO has come out in full support of liberalisation under GATS. The UNWTO takes its role of advocating for the tourism sector very seriously, and following the 2003 trade meetings in Mexico, the UNWTO chastised trade negotiators for the fact that agreement on agriculture was secured while tourism was neglected at these talks despite the fact that tourism makes a greater contribution to world trade (UNWTO, 2003a). In its press release, the UNWTO emphasised that liberalisation through GATS would boost the economies of the "world's poorer nations" by expanding "North-South flows", while "developed countries would not lose anything either because their enterprises will [sic] benefit from increased trade resulting from greater liberalization" (UNWTO, 2003a).

The UNWTO bases its claim that liberalisation of tourism helps poorer nations on the fact that as an export, tourism provides jobs and investment and that poorer nations are likely to attract higher tourism growth rates than developed countries because their underdevelopment means they have more pristine and exotic natural and cultural attractions. This argument ignores the high leakage factor in tourism in developing countries[70] and contradicts the view of such NGOs as Equations which regard the liberalisation agenda a serving the interests of the business sector. Indeed, the UNWTO does not recognise the more fundamental question of the unequal status of developing countries to developed countries (and the TNCs who lobby and set their agendas) in negotiations. This discrepancy has been recognised by UNCTAD and NGOs such as Equations which have raised it as a major source of concern. A comment on the Doha talks of 2001 by Mowforth and Munt illustrates what this unequal status looks like "on the ground":

> The mechanism for reaching agreement by consensus appears to be given as a major justification of GATS. But whether genuine consensus was achieved at the Doha Ministerial meeting in Qatar in November 2001, called to discuss GATS, or at previous similar meetings, is highly debatable: for instance, the 481 delegates from the G7 nations present at the Doha meeting was almost double the 276 delegates from the 39 Least Developed countries, and it is difficult if not impossible to achieve consensus agreement in such

---

[70] Crick's description of the leakages seen in developing countries is succinct and useful as he argues that vertical integration between airlines, hotel chains, travel agencies, rental car companies, etc. sees the TNC retain the majority of tourist spending and the "host" community receive very little. This is even worse with "all-inclusives" which are packaged holidays where the tourists pays for transport, accommodation, food and services in advance so that "much foreign exchange does not even reach the destination country" (1989, p. 316). In some countries leakages can be as high as 90%; Caribbean nations average 70% leakage (Patullo, 1996, p. 38). In the latter case, this means for every dollar earned in foreign exchange, 70 cents is lost to pay for imports.

unbalanced circumstances… in general, the GATS appears to reflect and reinforce rather that challenge the existing unevenness and inequality in the global economic system (2003, p. 266).

As Vellas and Becherel argue, the liberalisation of tourism under the GATS will indeed "contribute to the global development of tourism" (1995, pp. 268-269), but its effect can be translated as contributing to the growth and expansion of the tourism sector with the bulk of benefits accruing to the TCC and TNCs of the tourism sector. The GATS agreement is well set to deliver the continuous growth that the TCC and TNC supporters of capitalist globalisation seek to ensure for their ongoing profit and wealth accumulation. Whether the GATS delivers on the promises made to developing countries is another question.

3.5.2. More TNPs - Vertical Integration and Leveraging

Despite the fact that the majority of tourism businesses operating around the globe are SMEs, tourism is perhaps one of the most consolidated industries operating in the global community. Large TNCs such as TUI A. G.,[71] Thomas Cook, Hilton Hotels and British Airways dominate the international tourism and travel sector. Horizontal and vertical integration characterise the dynamics of tourism TNCs most of which originate from developed countries. Airlines invest in travel agencies, tour operators, computer reservation systems, accommodation as well as other airlines in an effort to extract more profit by dominating the sector and dictating terms. A good example is the Thomas Cook group, the third largest tourism and travel group in the world, which owns airlines, travel agencies, tour operations, foreign exchange bureaus, a publishing house and a television channel.[72]

---

[71] TUI A. G. describes itself thus: "TUI has an excellent position in its core tourism business. With a turnover of around Euro 13.1 billion, the Group is the unchallenged market leader in Europe. The European tour operators within World of TUI reach over 80 per cent of European holidaymakers. In 2004, the Group had around 18 million customers. TUI now includes about 3,200 travel agencies, more than 100 aircraft, 37 incoming agencies and 290 hotels with 163,000 beds in 28 countries. Around 12,000 business travel professionals in over 80 countries also look after the Group's business customers" (see: http://www.tui.com/en/ir/group/brief_portrait/).

[72] For an excellent insight into the Thomas Cook group see its corporate website at http://www.thomascook.com/ corporate/press.asp?page=presspack. Specifically, the company tells why it has pursued a path of vertical integration which has resulted in its formidable position:

"A vertically integrated company usually owns all or many areas of the value chain, including the supplier, the manufacturer and the retailer. In the case of travel companies, the supplier is the

Badger, Barnett, Corbyn and Keefe have claimed:

> power is increasingly in the hands of these large northern-based companies, who can direct flows of international tourists to particular destinations because of their high-tech globalised reservation systems. An estimated 80 per cent of all tourists travel with a tour operator package, so it is easy to appreciate the power of the tour operator vis-à-vis the host country (1996, p. 22).

The impacts of such a situation are not negligible and reveal much about the dynamics of capitalist globalisation. For instance, in 2003 the UK's Kuoni Travel asked 200 Asia-Pacific tourism suppliers to cut their rates by twenty percent in the high season in order to stimulate an economic recovery in the tourism sector following the downturns caused by SARS and security concerns (Colson, 2003). Kuoni's plan was to offer a "dedicated Far East special offer brochure" with bookings conducted in the September to March high season and it invited its suppliers in the region to agree. Both Thailand and Hong Kong tourism managers and operators reportedly responded negatively questioning whether Kuoni was bullying and taking advantage of circumstances for corporate profits (Colson, 2003; Sinclair, 2003). Perhaps bullying is evident in Kuoni's communications with Thailand representatives when Francis Torrilla, chief of products for Kuoni, claimed "Thailand's position as the number one destination for [Kuoni] was being challenged by the Maldives" (Colson, 2003). Colson claims that actual growth figures for the UK outbound market did not support Torrilla's statement and so it would seem that the Kuoni representative was manipulating the precarious position and intense competition between developing countries to intimidate Thai tourism managers into accepting Kuoni's "request". Such cases demonstrate the power exercised through TNPs which underpin the corporatised tourism system and enable the TCC and TNCs to reap profits and secure their interests to the

---

transport company (e.g. the airline) and/or the accommodation unit; the manufacturer is the tour operator who buys supplier components in bulk and produces the 'package holiday'; and the retailer is either a travel shop, a call centre or a website.

By creating this structure, a travel company has the advantage of influencing the distribution of its products and services to make sure that profits stay 'in-house'. Benefits to the consumer include better prices through the economies of scale that are achieved through more efficient buying, a one-stop shop for all travel products and services and a consistent level of customer service throughout the supply chain".

Unfortunately the benefits for the company and the tourists also coincide with losses and negative impacts for the host community and its national service suppliers.

detriment of the developmental capacities of tourism.[73] Another less obvious tourism TNP to address is the practise of global marketing of tourism through UN declared international years such as the 1967 International Year of Tourism, the 2002 International Year of Ecotourism and the 2002 International Year of Mountains. We now turn to a case study of the International Year of Ecotourism 2002 to demonstrate how such events are used to secure the corporatised tourism system.

3.5.3. International Year of Ecotourism 2002 - Celebration or Review?

The International Year of Ecotourism 2002 (IYE 2002) was designated by the United Nations Economic and Social Council (ECOSOC) in 1998 (through resolution 1998/40) to highlight the potential of ecotourism to contribute to economic development and environmental conservation. The UN Environment Program (UNEP) and the UNWTO were jointly assigned oversight, in partnership with three "northern" NGOs, the International Ecotourism Society (TIES), Conservation International (CI) and Ecological Tourism Europe (ETE) (Vivanco, 2001). In advising the direction of IYE 2002 activities, ECOSOC called upon the Secretary-General of the UN together with the UNEP, UNWTO and the WTTC to compile a report at the close of IYE 2002 activities detailing:

a.   Programmes and activities undertaken by Governments and interested organizations during the Year;
b.   An assessment of the results achieved in realizing the aims and objectives of the Year, particularly in terms of encouraging ecotourism in developing countries;
c.   Recommendations to further advance the promotion of ecotourism within the framework of sustainable development (ECOSOC, 1998).

These aims reflect an agenda of promotion and expansion of ecotourism. By combining the UNEP with the UNWTO, the UN was apparently hoping to underscore how ecotourism combines the need for economic development with environmental protection and conservation. However one also can see the origins of the dual and competing aims of the IYE 2002 initiative in this combination; the

---

[73] See Wahab and Cooper (2001a) for an academic analysis of the pressure on large tourism companies to vertically, horizontally and diagonally integrate in a globalised and competitive economic context and brief case studies of Germany, France and the United Kingdom.

UNEP is charged with ensuring environmental protection while the UNWTO, as argued earlier, is focused upon fostering tourism development and growth - ideally within the bounds of sustainability if the rhetoric is accepted at face value. One might think the balance in the program tips in favour of the "eco" in "ecotourism" given the involvement of the three environmental NGOs: TIES, CI and ETE in the IYE 2002 program, but Pleumarom has charged "corporate industry and large nature conservation/ecotourism organizations have colluded to lobby for the UN endorsement of ecotourism and now want to exploit it for self-serving purposes (e.g. to get free promotion or funding for their projects)" (2000).[74] Vivanco also refers to a 2000 meeting on the Convention of Biological Diversity where TIES was criticised "as one of the large nature conservation and development organizations that has consistently ignored local peoples' concerns in its drive to promote ecotourism" (2001). Additionally, the Rethinking Tourism Project (RTP)[75] representing Indigenous peoples charged "that international environmental NGOs and ecotourism organizations will benefit financially from the IYE - not communities" (RTP, 2000).[76] Whereas the involvement of TIES, CI and ETE in the IYE 2002 program was presented as a sign of good collaboration with the NGO sector in the development of the event, numerous less powerful NGOs which are much more critical of tourism could have been consulted and were not. This led to the charge that the IYE project was developed "behind closed doors". In fact, the promoters of the IYE 2002 initiative were accused of prematurely and uncritically "celebrating" ecotourism, despite its alleged dubious record.[77]

As a result, this initiative came in for early criticism from the NGOs fostering a developing country perspective on these events. The Tourism Investigation and Monitoring Team (TIM-Team) of the Third World Network (TWN), a non-governmental organisation representing views from the "South", called for "an international year of reviewing ecotourism" because they suspected the IYE 2002 to be a public relations exercise rather than a thorough review of the difficulties as well as the benefits of ecotourism and because of the non-transparent manner in

---

[74] Beder is useful in explaining the effect of capitalist globalisation on large environmental groups. See her book *Global spin: The corporate assault on environmentalism* (2000).

[75] RTP is now known as Indigenous Tourism Rights International (ITRI).

[76] RTP also specifically charged CI with opposing any criticism of ecotourism at the 1999 meetings of the Convention on Biological Diversity (RTP, 2000).

[77] For instance, see the TIES website where the IYE 2002 is discussed in terms of "celebration" (http://www.ecotourism.org/index2.php?about).

which the initiative came about (TIM-Team, no date b).[78] As preparations for the IYE 2002 began, the TIM-Team made a representation to the UN which stated:

> In the process [of developing IYE 2002], a clear division has developed between actors favouring promotion and commercialization of ecotourism as a major goal of the IYE, and a growing worldwide movement of public interest and indigenous peoples organizations that reject IYE as a promotional and business-oriented campaign"(TIM-Team, no date b).

The TIM-Team said that because the various stakeholders in ecotourism held divergent views on, definitions of and interests in ecotourism,[79] the coordinating bodies of the UNWTO and UNEP were incapable of establishing clear representative guidelines and objectives for the year. As a result the TIM-Team recommended that the UN General Assembly set the guidelines on the content and process of the IYE 2002 (particularly involving civil society stakeholders in tourism); that the event be geared to the public interest (i.e. ecological integrity, economic equity, social justice and human rights) and not be dominated by business interests; and that the IYE 2002 be focused on critical "reviewing" of ecotourism (TIM-Team, no date b). A gathering of over 1500 representatives of NGOs, people's movements and tribal communities in India in 2001, submitted a resolution to the UN claiming that the IYE 2002 is meant to "boost the eco tourism industry" and calling attention to the dangers of the IYE 2002 for developing countries and Indigenous peoples. Particular mention was made of its potential to continue the dynamics of dispossession, environmental damage (such as habitat destruction and loss of biodiversity) and stealing of Indigenous knowledge about medicinal plants by a profit-driven biotechnology industry (Sub-resolution on the UN IYE-2002, 2001).

Arguing that ecotourism particularly threatens the interests of Indigenous peoples, representatives of Indigenous peoples from around the world gathered in Oaxaca, Mexico in March 2002 to discuss Indigenous tourism and respond to the IYE 2002 initiative. This resulted in the Oaxaca Declaration in which they voiced their concerns and stated that "besides destroying the natural environments in which we live, tourism threatens traditional life by permanently altering the social, cultural and economic systems on which we depend" (Tourism Concern, 2002).

---

[78] Such activities as the use of World Bank Social Investment Project funding for inappropriate and illegal ecotourism development in Thai protected areas mentioned earlier provide reasons for the TIM-Team's suspicion of the ecotourism agenda (see TIM-Team, no date a).

[79] For instance, environmentalists emphasise conservation, hosts communities emphasise control and industry emphasises access and promotion.

Any assumption that the potential damage inflicted by the IYE 2002 would be limited to the short duration of the program was challenged by some critics of the initiative. For instance, Nina Rao speaking as the Southern co-chair of the NGO Tourism Caucus at the UN Commission for Sustainable Development (CSD) said "I really think this is going to be worse than the launch of package tours to the Third World" (cited in Pleumarom, 2000). The coalition of NGOs and other social movements clearly saw the IYE 2002 in terms of an aggressive campaign by the corporate interest against public welfare: "As nature-based tourism is presently seen as one of the most lucrative niche markets, powerful transnational corporations are likely to exploit the International Year of Ecotourism to dictate their own definitions and rules of ecotourism on society, while people-centred initiatives will be squeezed out and marginalized" (cited in Pleumarom, 2000).

The IYE 2002 can also be viewed as a catalyst to the "growth fetish" of capitalist globalisation where ecotourism is touted to be a tool for economic development and ecological protection for all countries around the globe. This gives the big TNCs an excuse, in conjunction with liberalisation initiatives such as GATS, to gain access to the markets of the developing world where tourism is seeing unprecedented growth rates. Pleumarom challenges the assumption that such developments can actually improve the situation of communities of the developing world as oversupply of ecotourism opportunities is likely to result and those who responded to the siren's call of the UNWTO and UNEP will find themselves critically worse off (Pleumarom, 1999a, 2000).[80] Factors such as debt incurred to develop ecotourism facilities and operations, the securing of TNC foreign investment on unfavourable terms (economically, socially and environmentally) and the abandonment of subsistence pursuits are all ways in which communities may secure worse outcomes from their engagement with the ecotourism phenomenon.

Academic Luis Vivanco has also provided extensive analysis of the IYE 2002 initiative (2001). His critique is perhaps one of the most extensive and well-argued. He concurs that the IYE 2002 initiative bears the hallmarks of a marketing campaign and demonstrates little of the critical reflection that ecotourism calls for. For instance, he makes a rarely insightful comment on one of the main hypocrisies underlining ecotourism in a capitalist context: "ecotourism rarely, if ever, calls

---

[80] Pleumarom provides the following example: "According to an article in the Bangkok newspaper *The Nation* (7 Apr. 1999), a comprehensive community development programme, initiated by His Majesty the King in the midst of economic woes, aims to develop eco-tourism - along with other economic activities such as farm produce processing, medicinal herb planting and traditional Thai medicine – in 15,223 villages, involving more than 300,000 families and a population of more than 700,000! This raises the question of oversupply in the face of unpredictable demand, a common hazard in the tourism industry" (1999a).

into question the consumption-oriented lifestyles that motivate ecotourists to travel in the first place" (2002). Importantly for this discussion, Vivanco sees wider dynamics evident in the IYE 2002 debates:

> At the very least, these critics are challenging the IYE's uncritical foundation on the market-driven and globalist mythologies of sustainable development, while offering alternative ways to think about and engage in tourism. They also exhibit trends in the broader anti-globalization mobilizations of recent years: the emergence of politically and culturally pluralistic coalitions operating in decentralized and horizontal fashion, imagining and generating non-prescriptive alternatives at both place-based and translocal scales (Vivanco, 2001).

Vivanco shows how the developments that Sklair and Gill witness in the arena of capitalist globalisation are also playing out in similar fashion in the realm of corporate tourism. But before we turn to the ways in which corporate tourism, like its sister capitalist globalisation, engender opposition because of their ecological and social impacts (and thereby generate the need for alternatives), it is first necessary to briefly examine the way in which the culture-ideology of consumerism can be identified within the tourism realm.

3.6. CULTURE-IDEOLOGY OF CONSUMERISM AND THE RIGHT TO TRAVEL

Conventional wisdom of current societies sees consumption as an expression of individuality and freedom. Hall suggests that such a perspective is misleading as tourism and leisure consumption in capitalist systems is increasingly commodified, standardised and industrialised; he asserts "the ideology of 'consumer sovereignty' disguises the extent to which capital controls leisure" (1994, pp. 192-193). According to Sklair, the culture-ideology of consumerism is a key linchpin of capitalist globalisation (2002). As Sklair states "consumerism has nothing to do with satisfying biological needs, for people will seek to satisfy these needs without any prompting from anyone, but with creating what can be called induced wants" (2002, p. 166). Tourism is a good example of consumerism as it is clearly one of these "induced wants". It is mostly a hedonistic leisure activity and is thus an item of optional consumption which the advertising profession and tourism industry continually tells us we need. In this era of capitalist globalisation and market rule, the privileged tourists are able to fulfil their desires while the less privileged work as their "servers" or "hosts".[81] Two aspects of the culture-ideology of consumerism evident in travel and tourism will be explored here: the psychological impact on the "consumer" or the tourist and the neo-imperialistic nature of the relationship it creates between the tourists and the toured or "hosts".

Firstly, the culture-ideology of consumerism operating in the tourism arena has very interesting psychological and sociological impacts on potential tourists and their societies. In addressing consumerism, Sklair uses the phrase "the great project of global consumerism" (2002, p. 196) which an individual can buy into through the small purchase of a can of cola or the more illusive holiday under discussion here. This reveals the psychological and sociological effects of current consumerism, that is the individual "buys into" consumerist society and asserts their identity no longer through citizenship but through consuming. Thus for the consuming individual, participating in consumerism goes to the heart of personal and social identity; you are literally nobody if you cannot assert your identity and belonging through your consumption practices. These dynamics also hold true in the contemporary tourism realm. A psychotherapist contributing to the travel section of the *Guardian* newspaper put our current conceptualisation of the right to travel in perspective when he questioned why holidays have become so important to people:

> Of course, it's because of expectations, affluence, the media, peer pressure, a shrinking world, etc. You could even say a kind of brainwashing. We feel that we deserve a holiday. In fact, we deserve two or three. Obviously, this has a lot to do with the availability of cheaper travel, and the growth in the time that exists, or we think should exist, for recreation and pleasure. But if you need something in order to be OK, then next time you will need more (Kirsh, 2003).

It is this dissatisfaction, the fact that "next time you will need more", that drives the culture and ideology of consumerism that underpins capitalist globalisation. The more one experiences, the more one needs and this contributes to the growing profits of the TNCs and serves the interests of the TCC. The inherent dissatisfaction found in consumerism is what spurs the "growth fetish" that Hamilton has found as the most important dynamic of our market system (2003).

---

[81] As Hall notes, tourism consumption is intimately related to class structures which results in a hierarchy of holiday experiences and holiday spaces (1994, pp. 194-195). He states "tourism is therefore very much part of the competition for and consumption of scarce resources..." (Hall, 1994, p. 195).

Perhaps a sign of the potential pathologies fostered by the culture-ideology of consumerism is the recent phenomenon seen in the UK where parents, particularly single mothers, abandon their children to go on holiday.[82] One mother trying to explain her actions to a woman's magazine stated "Everyone needs to let their hair down. My kids want for nothing. They have a wardrobe full of clothes and an attic full of toys" ("Holidaying Mother Charged with Neglect", 2005). One might choose to condemn this as an act of individual selfishness, but a considered analysis of the role of the culture-ideology of the right to travel is also called for. Advertising in all of its forms publicises that we all have a right to consume and holiday and somehow makes us feel less than adequate as people if we cannot. Could this make the underprivileged, of whom single-mothers in developed societies are a clear component, feel desperate to participate in consumer activities in order to give meaning to life and a sense of participation in the "good life" that living in capitalist societies most often denies them?

As Sklair cautions, it is easy to fall into a trap of moralising about what is or is not proper and acceptable consumption but that is not the point of his analysis of the culture-ideology of consumerism (2002, p. 187). The point of such an analysis is to demonstrate that under capitalist globalisation these induced wants are pressured upon people by a relentless torrent of "brainwashing" - pervasive media outlets constantly bombard us with billboard ads on the way to work, commercial television and radio, "women's magazines", film and music. Concerned with the impacts of the culture-ideology of consumerism on the developing world, Sklair contends that "the culture-ideology of consumerism creates a form of cultural dependency" and quotes Elizabeth Cardova's ironic definition: "Cultural dependency means people in our country have to brush their teeth three times a day, even if they don't have anything to eat" (Sklair, 2002, p. 187). What we see with the "children abandoned for holiday" phenomenon is that the inequities and pathologies of the culture-ideology of consumerism are not limited to the developing world; it is in effect wherever capitalist globalisation holds sway.

As the privileged assert their right to tourism and travel to the less expensive and more exotic destinations of the developing world, the ideology of the right to travel can be characterised as a neo-imperialist phenomenon; the privileged assert their rights while the poor and the marginalised serve and host them on their

---

[82] For instance see reports such as "Holidaying mother charged with neglect" at http://society.guardian.co.uk/ children/story/0,,1534310,00.html.; "Mum jailed for leaving kids behind" at http://society.guardian. co.uk/print/0,3858,5088424-108861,00.html; and " Mother abandons three children in squalor to go on holiday" at http://www.childalert.co.uk/absolutenm/templates/ newstemplate.asp? articleid=135&zoneid=1.

holidays in order to eke out a living and try to pay off the debts fostered by capitalist globalisation. This is well described by Bauman who claims the tourists "pay for their freedom; the right to disregard native concerns and feelings, the right to spin their own web of meanings... The world is the tourist's oyster... to be lived pleasurably - and thus given meaning" (1993, p. 241). Tourism under capitalist globalisation makes the world's places and peoples a product for consumption; "for the twentieth-century tourist, the world has become one large department store of countrysides and cities" (Schivelbusch, 1986, p. 197). As part of this equation, developing countries are cajoled and pressured into catering to tourists through the pressures of debt and the need for capital, with the result that practically no community is able to completely extricate itself from the tourism circuit.[83]

The ambiguities and perceived imposed nature of tourism on some communities is poignantly exposed by a Balinese academic who described the Bali bombing of 2002 as a "good thing" because it would stop foreign tourists from coming to Bali temporarily and give the Balinese a chance to reconsider their engagement with mass tourism and perhaps even persuade some to return to traditional and subsistence activities (Ellis, 2002, p. 4). While we could blame the imposition of tourism on vulnerable host societies upon the tourists or upon the governments who offer their people up to the tourism marketplace, MacCannell's (1992) analysis indicates this might not be a sufficient explanation. In his discussion of the "performative primitive" or "ex-primitive", MacCannell shows that many people from host communities who find themselves on the tourism circuit willingly engage with tourism and play the role the tourists expect (1992, p. 30). They are not the "exploited" peoples that unsophisticated tourism critics describe since they willingly engage with tourism as a way of accessing the goods and services of the capitalistic economy. For MacCannell, the exploitation lies in the "cannibalism" of capitalist globalisation which forces a "cannibal incorporation" as everyone, both tourist and "performative primitive", is forcibly brought into the capitalistic system; "the corporations promote this 'inevitable incorporation' with an aggressiveness that can only be labelled 'savage'" (1992, p. 68).

---

[83] Crick puts tourism consumption in a capitalist context in useful perspective: "tourism is the conspicuous consumption of resources accumulated in secular time; its very possibility, in other words, is securely rooted in the real world of gross political and economic inequalities between nations and classes. In fact... tourism is doubly imperialistic; not only does it make a spectacle of the Other, making cultures into consumer items, tourism is also an opiate of the masses in the affluent countries themselves (Crick cited in Hall, 1994, p. 196).

Table 2. Sklair's (1999) model of the sociology of the global system applied to tourism

TRANSNATIONAL PRACTICES	LEADING INSTITUTIONS	INTEGRATING AGENTS (e.g.)
Economic sphere • GATS • Consolidation, vertical integration	Economic forces • Global TNCs (eg. *TUI A.G., Thomas Cook*) • World Bank	Global Business Elite • Conrad Hilton, founder of Hilton Hotels • Richard Branson, founder of the Virgin conglomerate.
Political sphere • International Year of Eco- tourism 2002	Political forces • IATA, PATA • UNWTO, WTTC • Tourism Australia	Global Political Elite • Geoffrey Lipman, special adviser to UNWTO
Culture-ideology sphere • Right to travel	Culture-ideology forces • Travel agencies, media (*Conde Naste, Getaway*) • Publishers (*Lonely Plane*t) Social movements (*responsibletravel.com*)	Global Cultural Elite • Tony Wheeler, founder of Lonely Planet publications • Michael Palin, travel writer and presenter

The analysis of the culture-ideology of consumerism as expressed in the right to travel and tourism asserted in an era of corporatised tourism thus points to a system that parallels Sklair's "sociology of the global system". Table 2 applies Sklair's conceptualisation of capitalist globalisation to corporatised tourism. [84] A consumer ideology is first fostered in the tourists by promoting the right to travel and tourism. The "consumer" demand for tourism thus triggered is reinforced by the activities of governments, the TCC, TNCs and global institutions who seek to use this consumerism as a base for a corporatised tourism system. Many governments are coerced or compelled to get their communities to "host" these tourists through the pressures of SAPs, the need for investment and the hopes of development. The TCC and their affiliated TNCs actively promote the corporatised tourism system in forums such as GATS, the IFIs and the UN in order to secure access to profits and opportunities throughout the global

---

[84] Refer back to Table 1 "Sociology of the global system" (p. 26).

community. Institutional structures such as the UNWTO and the WTTC foster the transnational practices that are instrumental to corporatised tourism under capitalist globalisation. In particular, they promote further liberalisation and foster the importance of the tourism sector while also wielding the rhetoric of sustainability and poverty alleviation particularly when opposition arises to their corporate agendas. These forces create a self-reinforcing system which has the capacity to assert and promote its own growth and longevity (or MacCannell's evocative "cannibal incorporation"). The system confirms the ideological assertion that it is a natural and "good" order to which there exist no other "reasonable" alternatives (see figure 1).

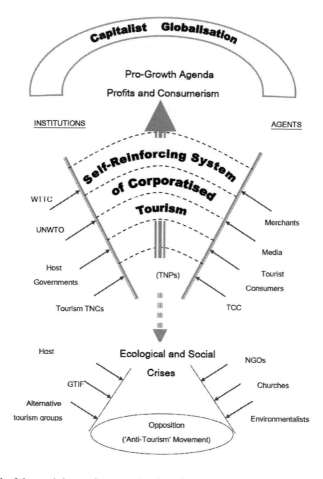

Figure 1. Model of the sociology of corporatised tourism.

However like its affiliated system capitalist globalisation, corporatised tourism is not entirely successful in this endeavour as it confronts opposition and resistance. This opposition arises from the damaging social and ecological effects of corporatised tourism akin to the critiques of capitalist globalisation (See figure 1).

3.7. EVIDENCE OF THE TWIN CRISES IN TOURISM

Sklair's theory of the sociology of globalisation posits that twin crises of class polarisation and ecological stress result from the processes and impacts of capitalist globalisation. The earlier discussion of the IYE 2002, and particularly Vivanco's succinct description of its dynamics, indicate that corporate tourism dynamics parallel uncannily the developments in capitalist globalisation witnessed by Sklair (2002). Is there further evidence of the twin crises in the realm of tourism?

International tourism, particularly between the developed and developing worlds, exhibits the tensions of class polarisation that Sklair has identified as an outcome of the dynamics of capitalist globalisation. Such tension is most evident between tourists and their hosts, as tourists display wealth and consumption patterns unimaginable to some of the inhabitants of the poorer regions to which tourists are increasingly drawn in their search for "authentic", "exotic" or "meaningful" experiences.[85] Such a situation is evident in the work of Hutnyk who investigated the "poverty tourism" found in Calcutta, India (1996). He describes the economic power displayed by poverty-gazing backpackers:

> The ability to move to conveniently inexpensive market and service centres through the facility of international travel yields a relatively high buying power with attendant ideological, habitual and attitudinal consequences - backpackers who can live like Rajas in Indian towns at low financial costs (Hutnyk, 1996, pp. 9-10).

---

[85] It should be noted that tourists often display consumption patterns on holiday that are not evident in their routine lives back home because they save or borrow for the annual holiday splurge. Often the hosts are not aware that the conspicuous consumption of tourists is only a fleeting occurrence and that quite burdensome work routines and stress levels are endured to temporarily enjoy the holiday lifestyle.

Such discrepancies in wealth, power and status are particularly apparent in the tourism encounter as the tourist often comes "face to face" with the poor.[86] Crick has described this as "leisure imperialism" and the "hedonistic face of neo-colonialism" (1989, p. 322). That resentment is fuelled by this situation is apparent in the crime, violence, corruption and hostility that is apparent in many international tourism destinations including Jamaica, India, Sri Lanka, Egypt and Indonesia.[87] For instance, in a rare case of journalism which sought to explain the roots of violence against tourists, Levy and Scott-Clark (2006) explain how rapid societal changes brought on by tourism development has fuelled a "violent crime wave" on the island of Koh Samui, Thailand. They note how this island moved from a sleepy backwater to hosting over one million tourists every year within the span of two decades and how foreign and elite interests have come to dominate tourism (Levy and Scott-Clark, 2006). Levy and Scott-Clark refer to a submission made by Thai academics to the Thai government which describes a "social and moral implosion" which has ensued as "fewer than 20% of islanders have benefited from the boom, leading to 'explosive tensions' between rich and poor residents, mainland Thais and foreigners" (2006). It is also readily apparent in the stories of Australian evacuees from New Orleans in the aftermath of hurricane Katrina in 2005, several of whom were threatened with physical violence if they were given "preferential treatment" by being evacuated before the poor (and mostly African-American) locals (Koch, 2005, p. 6).

The class polarisation generated by tourism under capitalism is more complex than the gulf between tourists and host communities. Tensions are also exacerbated between locals at the tourism destination as different groups are affected differently by the onset of tourism. Tensions pit youth against elders and local elites against the masses (Dogan, 1989). Crick claims:

> Benefits from tourism 'unlike water, tend to flow uphill'...the profits go to the elites – those already wealthy, and those with political influence...the poor find themselves unable to tap the flow of resources while the wealthy need only use their existing assets (e.g. ownership of well-positioned real estate, political influence) to gain more (1989, p. 317).

Under the international tourism system, smaller tourism operators and those from the informal sector find themselves competing with larger and more powerful interests, particularly the transnational corporations in the era of

---

[86] Britton has stated "no printed page, broadcast speech, or propaganda volley can emphasise the inequity in the global distribution of wealth as effectively as tourism can" (cited in Crick, 1989, p. 317).

[87] See Dogan's analysis of the socio-cultural impacts of tourism (1989).

liberalisation. The interests of these SMEs and informal service providers are not supported or protected by the local elites and governmental authorities who, as local affiliates of the TCC, respond to the dictates of capitalist globalisation and not to the imperatives of national development. In fact, tourism can result in violation of the human rights of beggars, street children and hawkers who are seen as "human litter" and as "so much refuse spoiling things for visitors" (Crick, 1989, p. 317). The aftermath of the Asian tsunami of December 2004 illustrates some of these dynamics in a palpable way. Nesiah alleges that affected governments have collaborated with the tourism industry to secure corporate interests rather than rehabilitation of local communities:

> From Thailand to Sri Lanka, the tourist industry saw the tsunami through dollar signs. The governments concerned were on board at the outset, quickly planning massive subsidies for the tourism industry in ways that suggest the most adverse distributive impact. Infrastructure development will be even further skewed to cater to the industry rather than the needs of local communities. Within weeks of the tsunami, the Alliance for the Protection of Natural Resources and Human Rights, a Sri Lankan advocacy group, expressed concern that 'the developing situation is disastrous, more disastrous than the tsunami itself, if it is possible for anything to be worse than that' (Nesiah, 2005).

Nesiah tells how Sri Lankan civil society has a long history of opposition to governments that had readily implemented neoliberal agendas demanded under poverty reduction strategy papers (formerly SAPs). The NGOs of Sri Lankan civil society are gearing up for a huge fight as the government stands accused of displacing coastal dwellers such as "fisherfolk", ostensibly for their safety, while in fact zoning for major tourism facilities which will ensure their displacement (Nesiah, 2005). Nesiah describes it thus: "ultimately, it looks like reconstruction will be determined by the deadly combination of a rapacious private sector and government graft: human tragedy becomes a commercial opportunity, tsunami aid a business venture" (2005). This is the inexorable logic of capitalist globalisation put in a nutshell and it stands in marked contrast to what redevelopment could have looked like in Sri Lanka if the prevailing logic had been that of a grassroots-needs driven globalisation based on human rights as envisioned by Sklair (2002).

The evidence on the ecological impacts of tourism is wide-ranging and is perhaps a key feature of the tourism literature critiquing the impacts of tourism (e.g. Cater and Goodall, 1997; Duffy, 2002; Gossling, 2002a, 2002b; Pleumarom, 1999a, 1999b, 1999c, 1999d). Does tourism threaten an ecological crisis comparable to that described by Sklair in his discussion of capitalist globalisation? It is difficult to mount a case that tourism contributes to a crisis because tourism is only one force among the multitude that comprises capitalist globalisation. Thus it is difficult to assert that its impacts on the natural environment are as substantial as the insatiable demands for natural resources that are required to create the consumer products that feed the growth of capitalism. In fact, one of the arguments of bodies such as the UNWTO and UNEP in fostering the IYE 2002 was that ecotourism in particular is an environmentally more benign development choice. However, evidence of damage to coral reefs, soil erosion in alpine environments, deforestation along tourism treks, marine pollution from cruising, noise pollution from marine recreation, introduction of feral species, loss of biodiversity, piling up of solid wastes, ground water depletion, sewerage pollution of water and food sources and curtailing of alternative land uses such as wilderness or agriculture are amongst numerous other negative impacts in places all around the globe that provide anecdotal evidence that the ecological pressures of tourism are considerable if not already describable as a full-blown crisis. Surveys such as Margolis' (2006) suggest that tourism pressure on sites around the world is increasingly worrying. [88] He reports that Conservation International has identified "unsustainable tourism" as the main threat to 50% of heritage sites in Latin America and the Caribbean and 20% of sites in Asia and the Pacific (Margolis, 2006). The recent experience of devastation from the Asian tsunami is indicative of what can result from tourism's negative impacts on the environment. It is alleged that tourism and other developments throughout the Indian Ocean basin damaged and undermined coral reefs and mangrove systems which could have provided some buffer against the waves that pounded the shorelines of the Maldives, Sri Lanka, Thailand and India in particular and perhaps prevented such large losses of life (Nesiah, 2005; Sharma, 2005). Controversially, some have also connected these developments to the wider phenomenon of global warming as reefs are killed and rising waters erode shorelines and coastal defences (Thibault, 2004). Similarly the devastation of hurricane Katrina was allegedly magnified by the loss of wetlands and damage to the Mississippi delta due to urban development.

Whether these allegations are valid or not, perhaps one of the easiest charges on which to indict tourism is its contribution to the global warming phenomenon.

---

[88] Margolis identifies endangered sites around the globe, including Venice, Stonehenge, the Tower of London, the Great Wall of China, Macchu Pichu, Cancun, Angor Wat, the Taj Mahal, the snows of Kilimanjaro, New Orleans and Antarctica as attractions in danger of vanishing either due to the attracting of hordes of tourists or the indirect impacts of tourism such as the effects of global warming (2006). Margolis' byline reads "the world's treasures are under siege as never before. So get out and see as many as possible before they disappear" (2006).

While the scientific community debates this issue vociferously, prompted perhaps by "corporate-sponsored confusion",[89] some of those most likely impacted, including some governments and insurance companies, seem to be treating the issue seriously. It is apparent that transport and travel are key contributors to global warming and obviously the tourism sector would be a major consumer for its use of cars in domestic tourism and of aviation in international tourism.

The United Kingdom has been one of the most active countries in the global community to deal with this issue and provides some helpful information to evaluate the impacts of air travel on global environmental degradation. Under the Kyoto protocol only domestic aviation emissions are counted as part of a country's greenhouse gas reduction targets because agreement has not yet been reached on how to divide the emissions associated with international travel. The UK, however, includes both its domestic and international passenger and freight transport sectors in its calculations for reductions. With one in five international airline passengers travelling to or from a UK airport, the UK's interest in this issue is perhaps greater than most. As a result its Department of Transport has drafted a plan to use technical means to reduce this sector's contribution to global warming in order to assist in meeting the targets set in Kyoto in 1997 (Department of Transport, 2004). However, the Green Party has challenged such technical action as inadequate as aviation demand continues to grow sparked by the "growth fetish" of capitalism and because taxpayers are subsidising air transport through many hidden subsidies and costs (Whiteleg and Fitz-Gibbon, 2003). The Green Party's report "Aviation's Economic Downside" claims:

> The costs of UK aviation's contribution to climate change are estimated at well over £2 billion a year in 2001. And unless the government radically changes its policy on the matter, aviation's CO_2 emissions will have increased by 588% between 1992 and 2050, and its NOx pollution by 411%. By 2050, aviation could be contributing up to 15% of the overall global warming effect produced by human activities - with staggering economic costs (Whiteleg and Fitz-Gibbon, 2003).

This brief exploration into global warming shows that tourism does, indeed, play a significant contributing role. This explains why the UNWTO has supported the pronouncement of the Djerba Declaration on Tourism and Climate Change of 2003. But as Gossling and Hall note "air travel is the most important factor

---

[89] Beder alleges that corporations have sponsored the think tanks and foundations that have argued against global warming (2000, pp. 233-245).

negatively influencing tourism's environmental sustainability" (2006, p. 311). [90] To date the tourism industry has been unable to meaningfully address this threat to corporatised tourism's growth agenda.

3.8. OPPOSITION FOSTERED BY THE TWIN CRISES

As Sklair (2002) suggests, the crises that capitalist globalisation engenders undermine its future by raising implacable opposition from the "anti-globalisation" movement. This has been most evident at recent global gatherings of TNCs and the TCC convened under the auspices of bodies such as the WTO and WEF since Seattle in 1999. There are also more pro-active and constructive meetings of global civil society groups under the banner of the World Social Forum (WSF) held at the beginning of each year since 2001. The way this group describes itself shows that it clearly corresponds to Sklair's conceptualisation of a movement against capitalist globalisation and is in favour of a more human-centred alternative globalisation. A recent website states:

> Peoples' movements around the world are working to demonstrate that the path to sustainable development, social and economic justice lies in alternative models for people-centred and self-reliant progress, rather than in neo-liberal globalisation.
> The World Social Forum (WSF) was created to provide an open platform to discuss strategies of resistance to the model for globalisation formulated at the annual World Economic Forum at Davos by large multinational corporations, national governments, IMF, the World Bank and the WTO, which are the foot soldiers of these corporations.
> Firmly committed to the belief that Another World Is Possible the WSF is an open space for discussing alternatives to the dominant neo-liberal processes, for exchanging experiences and for strengthening alliances among mass organisations, peoples' movements and civil society organisations (World Social Forum, 2004).

---

[90] Gossling and Hall (2006, p. 314) document expert opinion that argues that the impacts of rapid climate change are more serious and a greater number of negative ecological consequences have resulted than early analysis predicted. Gossling and Hall's analysis of tourism's contribution to global climate change puts it on par with Sklair's prediction of an ecological crisis: "It would…be strangely ironic if the impact of tourism mobility also becomes the factor that leads to irreversible environmental change that will take not only many species and ecosystems with it, but possibly even humans themselves" (2006, p. 317).

The potential for tourism to undergo a similar trajectory to capitalist globalisation was noted by anthropologist Malcolm Crick as far back as 1989 when he suggested "perhaps tourism, like capitalism, has within it the seeds of its own destruction" (1989, p. 338). Because tourism engenders social and ecological crises as a result of its adverse impacts, it has received vocal and sustained criticism from both the NGO sector as well as a certain sociological segment in academia (Burns, 2005; Crick, 1989). However what we have not seen is sustained protest and resistance to tourism on a global scale that parallels the "anti-globalisation" movement since 1999. Perhaps this is because tourism's impacts are particularly local and so protests and opposition have focused on particular developments at particular times. However, this is no longer true. At the World Social Forum held in Mumbai in 2004, tourism was put on the agenda for the attention of global civil society and came in for concerted criticism. At the convened Global Summit on Tourism the theme was "Who really benefits from tourism?" and a call to "democratise tourism!" was released. One NGO participant, the Ecumenical Coalition on Tourism (ECOT) called for the WSF to advocate for a tourism that is "pro-people" (ECOT, 2003). Attendees at the meeting formed the Tourism Interventions Group (TIG)[91] and released a statement of concern which echoes the concerns of other new social movements opposing capitalist globalisation (TIG, 2004). TIG clearly positioned itself in opposition to capitalist globalisation and its affiliated corporatised tourism:

> We decided to strengthen and uphold the grassroots perspectives of tourism, which position our interventions against those of the World Tourism Organization (WTO-OMT) [UNWTO], the World Travel and Tourism Council (WTTC) and other mainstream definitions of tourism policy and development. As the WTO-OMT [UNWTO] is now a specialised UN agency, we will address its new mandate and take forward civil society engagements to democratise tourism.
> A primary concern is the undemocratic nature of the ongoing negotiations in the World Trade Organisation's General Agreement on Trade in Services (GATS) that are slated to end by January 2005. We stress the urgent need to bring in experiences from the grassroots on the environmental and social costs of tourism to inform the negotiating positions of governments and underline the need for a rollback in the negotiations (TIG, 2004).

---

[91] The TIG has since become more widely known as the Global Tourism Interventions Forum (GTIF).

However, the TIG also made very clear what its movement stood for and in doing so, resonated the aspirations of other new social movements participants gathered at the WSF. They claimed:

> Highlighting tourism issues within a multitude of anti-globalisation and human rights movements such as those related to women, children, dalits, indigenous people, migrants, unorganised labour, small island, mountain and coastal communities, as well as struggles related to land, water and access to natural resources, is crucial to sharpen local struggles and community initiatives of those impacted by tourism. Networking is at the core of future strategising to identify areas of common concern, forge alliances with like-minded individuals, organisations and movements and influence tourism policy agendas. Democracy, transparency and corporate and governmental accountability in tourism will be placed high on the agenda for concerted action and strategic interventions.
>
> We look forward to working in solidarity with local community representatives, activists and researchers from various parts of the world to strengthen our struggle and develop strategies for a tourism that is equitable, people-centred, sustainable, ecologically sensible, child-friendly and gender-just (TIG, 2004).[92]

This is a tall order, indeed, and brings to mind Sklair's description of socialist globalisation quoted previously:

> Socialist globalisation would eventually raise the quality of life (rather than the standards of living set by consumerist capitalism) of everyone and render the culture-ideology of consumerism superfluous by establishing less destructive and polarizing cultures and ideologies in its place. There is no blueprint for this – if we want such a world we will have to create it by trial and error (2002, p. 325).

We are witnessing this trial and error under way at the World Social Forum. Interestingly, activists perceive tourism as integral to this process. Certainly the institutionalisation of a movement for a more just form of tourism through the

---

[92] It should be noted that this tourism gathering at the 2004 WSF is not the only evidence of a global challenge to corporate tourism. Vivanco described the Indigenous Tourism Forum convened in Oaxaca, Mexico in 2002 to challenge the agenda of the IYE 2002 in a similar manner: "the participants therefore regard their growing relationships as a convivial space of intercultural dialogue and encounter, proceeding along mutually-constructed agenda that reject reduction of human experiences and development along a single line or within a single system. This interculturalism and pluralism offers a profound political challenge to globalist aspirations of ecotourism's and IYE's promoters and brings to the forefront questions of cultural and community survival in their deepest senses" (2001).

formation of the TIG provides an organisational structure with resources, power and influence which can carry out a sustained attack on the corporatised tourism system and oppose its social and environmental inequities. In light of the success of the French anti-globalisation NGO Attac in derailing the Multi-lateral Agreement on Investment in 1998 the threat posed by the GTIF to corporatised tourism should not be discounted.

Chapter 4

CONCLUSION

This book has devoted significant attention to the globalisation phenomenon because it is arguably establishing the parameters for contemporary social, economic and political action. While there is a diversity of opinions and viewpoints about the essence, import and impacts of globalisation, there is general agreement that it is a phenomenon worthy of study and analysis. However the argument presented here is that if concern is with sustainability, equity, justice and human welfare, then capitalist globalisation is the most vital aspect of globalisation to contend with. Leslie Sklair's model of capitalist globalisation was analysed in considerable detail because of the comprehensive and useful account it provides of the dynamics of contemporary capitalist globalisation. This chapter has applied Sklair's (2002) model of capitalist globalisation to contemporary tourism in order to reveal some of the qualities and impacts of corporatised tourism. It investigated the ways in which transnational actors such as the TCC and TNCs, transnational institutions such as the UNWTO and WTTC, transnational practices such as liberalisation under GATS and the culture-ideology of consumerism create a self-reinforcing system that seeks to secure the interests of the beneficiaries of corporatised tourism and sustain this system in the long term.

While tourism is demonstrably very powerful and is intimately tied to the processes of capitalist globalisation, it is also an agent for change wielded by organisations such as the Tourism Interventions Group that ironically may contribute to overturning this very form of globalisation. Just as Sklair noted that capitalist globalisation and its attendant crises make space for a socialist globalisation based on human rights, corporatised tourism's impacts and exploitation inspire challenges to develop a tourism that is "pro-people" and based on justice (ECOT, 2003).

It is apparent from this brief examination, that tourism management in the 21st century will be confronted with tensions and challenges. It is advisable that tourism managers critically evaluate the dynamics exposed in this analysis. Corporatised tourism's social and ecological damages potentially threaten the very future of tourism and necessitate an agenda of reform. Groups such as the TIG will be organised as effectively as their counterparts in the "anti-globalisation" movement to hold tourism leaders and proponents accountable for their impacts. While corporatised tourism, like capitalist globalisation, seems here to stay, this analysis suggests that it carries with it the "seeds of its own destruction" (Crick, 1989, p. 338). Shaping tourism to a more humane and ecologically sound form as we embark upon the 21st century may be one lesson that this analysis offers to tourism managers seeking a more successful and stable future.

REFERENCES

Abu-Lughod, J. (1991). Going beyond global babble. In A. D. King (Ed.). *Culture, globalization and the world system* (pp. 131-138). Minneapolis: University of Minnesota Press.

Appadurai, A. (1996). Disjuncture and difference in the global cultural economy. In A. Appadurai (Ed.). *Modernity at large: Cultural dimensions of globalization* (pp. 27-47). Minneapolis: University of Minnesota Press.

Badger, A., Barnett, P., Corbyn, L. and Keefe, J. (1996). *Trading places: Tourism as trade*. London: Tourism Concern.

Barber, B. (1996). *Jihad vs. McWorld*. New York: Ballentine Books.

Bauman, Z. (1993). *Postmodern ethics*. London: Routledge.

Beder, S. (2000). Global spin: The corporate assault on environmentalism. Melbourne: Scribe.

Bendell, J. and Font, X. (2004). Which tourism rules? Green standards and GATS. *Annals of Tourism Research*, 31(1), 139-156.

Bennholdt-Thomsen, V. and Mies, M. (1999). *The subsistence perspective: Beyond the globalised economy*. London: Zed Books.

Berne Declaration and Working Group on Tourism and Development. (2004). The WTO General Agreement on Trade in Services and sustainable tourism in developing countries - in contradiction? Retrieved 2 August 2005, from http://www.akte.ch/pages/en/4_news/_aktion/Tourismus%20and%20GATS%20englisch.pdf.

Britton, S. (1982). The political economy of tourism in the Third World. *Annals of Tourism Research*, 9(3), 331- 358.

Brohman, J. (1996). New directions in tourism for third world development. *Annals of Tourism Research*, 23(1), 48-70.

Burns, P. M. (1999). *An introduction to tourism and anthropology*. London: Routledge.

Burns, P. M. (2005). Social identities, globalisation, and the cultural politics of tourism. In W. F. Theobold (Ed.). *Global tourism* (3rd ed., pp. 391-405). Amsterdam: Elsevier.

Cater, E. and Goodall, B. (1997). Must tourism destroy its resource base? In L. France (Ed.). *Earthscan reader in sustainable tourism* (pp.85-89). London: Earthscan Publications.

Cohen, R. and Kennedy, P. (2000). *Global sociology*. Houndsmills, UK: Macmillan Press.

Colson, J. (2003). Kuoni UK outrages suppliers. *Travel Trade Gazette Asia*, July 25-July 31. Retrieved 2 August 2005, from http://www.twnside. org.sg/title2/ttcd/EG-02.doc.

Communication from the Dominican Republic, El Salvador and Honderas. (2000). *Replies to the comment on the proposed annex on tourism*. Retrieved 2 August 2005, http://www.wto.org/english/tratop_e/serv_e/special_ sessiondoc/w9.doc.

Communication from the Dominican Republic, El Salvador, Honderas, Nicaragua and Panama. (2000). *The cluster of tourism industries*. Retrieved 2 August 2005, from http://www.wto.org/english/tratop_e/serv_e/special_sessiondoc/w19.doc.

Cooper, C., Fletcher, J., Fyall, A., Gilbert, D. and Wanhill, S. (2005). *Tourism principles and practice* (3rd ed.). Essex: Pearson Education Ltd.

Cooper, Y. (2005, 22 March). Now we must narrow the wealth gap. *The Guardian*. Retrieved 1 March 2005, from http://www.guardian.co.uk/ comment/story/0,,1443099,00.html.

Crick, M. (1989). Representations of international tourism in the social sciences: Sun, sex, sights, savings, and servility. *Annual Review of Anthropology*, 18, 307-344.

Dangl, B. (2005). Occupy, resist, produce: Worker cooperatives in Buenos Aires. *Znet*, 3 March. Retrieved 19 December 2005, from http://www.zmag.org/content/showarticle.cfm?SectionID=42andItemID=735 3.

Davis, H. D. and Simmons, J. A. (1982). World Bank experience with tourism projects. *Tourism Management*, 3(4), 212-217.

Department of Transport. (2004). *Aviation and global warming*. Retrieved 16 September 2005, from http://www.dft.gov.uk/stellent/groups/dft_aviation/ documents/page/ dft_aviation_031850.pdf.

Diaz-Benavides, D. (2002). Worldwide tourism as an engine of sustainable development. Retrieved 2 August 2005, from http://www2.gtz.de/ tourismus/download/tfi2002/diaz.pdf.

Dogan, H. Z. (1989). Forms of adjustment: Sociocultural impacts of tourism. *Annals of Tourism Research*, 16, 216-236.

Duffy, R. (2002). *A trip too far*. London: Earthscan.

Ecumenical Coalition on Tourism. (2003). Concept paper for World Social Forum. Unpublished document.

Elliott, J. (1997). Tourism: Politics and public sector management. London: Routledge.

Ellis, E. (2002, 22 October). Cleansing of foreign evils a 'good thing'. *The Australian*, 4.

Equations. (2001). *Trade in tourism through the GATS: Interests of developing countries at stake*. Retrieved 16 August 2005, from http://www.zmag.org/ content/SouthAsia/ equations_tourism-gats.cfm.

Equations. (2002). *Weighing the GATS on a development scale: The case of tourism in Goa, India*. Retrieved 2 August 2005, from http://www.somo.nl/html/paginas/pdf/ Tourism_in_India_2002_EN.pdf.

Equations. (2004). Why the GATS is a wrong framework through which to liberalise tourism. Policy briefing paper to the WTO-OMT International symposium on trade in tourism services.

Fayos-Solá, E. and Bueno, A. P. (2001). Globalization, national tourism policy and international organizations. In S. Wahab and C. Cooper (Eds.). *Tourism in the age of globalisation* (pp. 45-65). London: Routledge.

Frank, A. G. (1996). The underdevelopment of development. In S. Chew and R. Denemark (Eds.). *The underdevelopment of development: Essays in honour of Andre Gunder Frank*. Thousand Oaks, CA: Sage Publications.

Friedman, T. (2000). *The lexus and the olive tree*. London: Harper Collins.

Giddens, A. (1986). *Sociology: A brief but critical introduction* (2nd ed.). Houndmills, UK: Macmillan.

Giddens, A. (1990). *The consequences of modernity*. Stanford, CA: Stanford University Press.

Giddens, A. (1999). Runaway world: How globalization is reshaping our lives. London: Profile Books.

Gill, S. (1995). Globalisation, market civilisation and disciplinary neoliberalism. *Millennium: Journal of International Studies*, 24 (3), 399-423.

Gill, S. (1999). Globalisation and crisis at the end of the twentieth century, Discussion Paper No. 26, May 7th, Centre for Development Studies, Flinders University of South Australia.

Gill, S. (2000a). The constitution of global capitalism. Paper presented to a Panel: The capitalist world, past and present at the International Studies Association Annual Convention, Los Angeles. Retrieved 11 April 2005, from http://www.theglobalsite.ac.uk/ press/010gill.htm.

Gill, S. (2000b). Towards a postmodern prince? The battle of Seattle as a moment in the new politics of globalization. *Millennium: Journal of International Studies*, 29(1), 131-140.

Goldstone, D. L. (2005). From pilgrimage to package tour: Travel and tourism in the Third World. New York: Routledge.

Gossling, S. (2002 a). Global environmental consequences of tourism. *Global Environmental Change*, 12, 283-302.

Gossling, S. (2002b). Human- environmental relations within tourism. *Annals of Tourism Research*, 29(2), 539-556.

Gossling, S. and Hall, C. M. (Eds.). (2006). Tourism and global environmental change: Ecological, social, economic and political interrelationships. London: Routledge.

Green Globe. (no date). Green Globe. Retrieved 12 July 1999, from http://www.wttc.org/greenglobe.

Green Travel. (1999). web discussion group, at Green-Travel@peach.ease.lsoft.com, communications from DaveK@iipt.org on 6 April 1999 on IIPT Glasgow conference.

Hall, C. M. (1994). *Tourism and politics: Policy, place and power*. Chichester, UK: John Wiley and Sons.

Hall, C. M. (2000). Tourism planning: Policies, processes and relationships. Harlow, UK: Prentice-Hall.

Hall, C. M. (2003). Politics and place: An analysis of power in tourism communities. In S. Singh, D. J. Timothy and R. K. Dowling (Eds.). *Tourism in destination communities* (pp. 99-114). Oxon, UK: CABI.

Hall, C. M. and Tucker, H. (2004). Tourism and postcolonialism: Contested discourses, identities and representations. Oxon, UK: Routledge.

Hamilton, C. (2003). *Growth fetish*. Crows Nest, NSW: Allen and Unwin.

Harnecker, C. P. (2006). If we don't try, we've already made a mistake. *New Internationalist*, 390, June, p. 11.

Harrison, D. (2001). Tourism and the less developed world: Issues and case studies. Oxon, UK: CABI.

Held, D. (no date). Globalization after September 11th. Retrieved 6 June 2003, from http://www.polity.co.uk/global/after_sept11.htm.

Held, D. and McGrew, A. (Eds.). (2000). The global transformations reader: An introduction to the globalization debate. Malden, MA: Polity Press.

Hellyer, P. (1999). *Stop: Think*. Toronto: Chimo Media.

Henderson, H. (1999). *Beyond globalization: Shaping a sustainable global economy*. West Hartford, CT: Kumarian Press.

Higgins-Desbiolles, F. (2006). More than an industry: The forgotten power of tourism as a social force. *Tourism Management*, 27, 1192-1208.

Hoad, D. (2002). The General Agreement on Trade in Services and the impact on trade liberalisation on tourism and sustainability. *Tourism and Hospitality Research*, 4(3), 213-227.

Hoenig, J. (2003). In defense of global capitalism. *Smartmoney.com*, 10 November. Retrieved 3 April 2006, from http://www.smartmoney.com/tradecraft/index.cfm?story=20031110.

Holidaying mother charged with neglect. (2005, 22 July). *The Guardian*. Retrieved 2 October 2005, from http://www.guardian.co.uk/child/story/0,,1534312,00.html.

Holton, R. J. (1998). *Globalization and the nation-state*. Basingstoke, UK: Macmillan.

Hoogvelt, A. (1997). Globalisation and the postcolonial world: The new political economy of development. Houndmills, UK: Macmillan Press.

Hutnyk, J. (1996). The rumour of Calcutta: Tourism, charity and the poverty of representation. London: Zed Books.

Jameson, F. (2001). Notes on globalization as a philosophical issue. In F. Jameson and M. Miyoshi (Eds.). *The cultures of globalization*. Durham, NC: Duke University Press.

Kalisch, A. (2001). *Tourism as fair trade: NGO perspectives*. London: Tourism Concern.

Khan, M. K. (1997). Tourism development and dependency theory: Mass tourism vs. ecotourism. *Annals of Tourism Research*, 24(4), 988-991.

Khor, M. (2003, 12 July). *Report on services talks: Developing countries sceptical on more liberalisation*. Retrieved 2 August 2005, from http://www.twnside.org.sg/eng.htm.

Khor, M. (2005, 4 July). North, south differ on service talks and need for new approach. Retrieved 1 February 2006, from http://www.twnside.org.sg/eng.htm.

Kirsh, M. (2003, 31 May). Making the most of it. *The Guardian*. Retrieved 6 September 2005, from http://travel.guardian.co.uk/activities/rest/story/0,8642,967322,00.html.

Klein, N. (2001). *No logo*. London: Flamingo.

Koch, T. (2005, 12 September) Backpackers thank Superdome saviour. *The Australian*, 6.

Kostigen, T. (2004). Growing wealth gap rates an 'orange alert': 'Inequality Matters' Conference puts nations on alert. Retrieved 1 March 2005, from http://www.commondreams.org/headlines04/0601-07.htm.

Lechner, F. J. and Boli, J. (Eds.). (2000). *Globalization reader*. Oxdford: Blackwell Publishers.

Leiper, N. (1995). *Tourism management*. Melbourne: RMIT Press.

Levy, A. and Scott-Clark, C. (2006, 8 April). Danger in paradise. *The Guardian*. Retrieved 15 May 2006, from http://www.guardian.co.uk/weekend/story/ 0,,1748146,00.html.

MacCannell, D. (1992). *Empty meeting grounds*. London: Routledge.

Margolis, M. (2006). Vanishing acts. *Newsweek* (online). Retrieved 5 May 2006, from http://www.msnbc.msn.com/id/12113285/site/newsweek/.

McLaren, D. (1998). *Rethinking tourism and ecotravel*. West Hartford, CT: Kumarian Press.

McLuhan, M. (1962). *The Gutenberg galaxy*. Toronto: University of Toronto Press.

McMichael, P. (1998). Demystifying globalisation, briefly. In M. Alexander, M. Alexander, S. Harding, P. Harrison, G. Kendall, Z. Skrbis and G. Western (Eds.). *Refashioning sociology: Responses to a new world order* (pp. 299-304). TASA Conference Proceedings, Brisbane. QUT Publications.

McMichael, P. (2000). *Development and social change*. Thousand Oaks, CA: Pine Forge Press.

Menotti, V. (2002). The World Trade Organization and ecotourism. First International Conference of Ecologist Mayors of Ecotourism, 22-24 November, Cancun Mexico. Retrieved 2 August 2005, from http://www.ifg.org/analysis/wto/cancun/etourvm.htm.

Mowforth, M. and Munt, I. (2003). Tourism and sustainability: Development and new tourism in the Third World (2nd ed.). London: Routledge.

Muqbil, I. (2006). No deal better that bad deal at the WTO. *Travel Impact Newswire*, 26 July.

Nash, D. (2000). Acculturation. In J. Jarari (Ed.). *Encyclopedia of tourism* (pp. 6-7). London: Routledge.

Nederveen Pieterse, J. (2000). Globalization as hybridization. In F. J. Lechner and J. Boli (Eds.). *Globalization reader* (pp. 99-108). Oxford: Blackwell Publishers.

Nesiah, V. (2005). Fisherfolk out, tourists in. *Dollars and Sense: The Magazine of Economic Justice*, Issue 260, July/August. Retrieved 16 September 2005, from http://www.dollarsandsense.org/0705nesiah.html.

New Internationalist. (2005). *The world guide*. Oxford: New Internationalist.

Norberg, J. (2003). *In defense of global capitalism*. Washington, DC: Cato Institute.

Noypayak, W. (2001). Thailand: Experiences in trade negotiations in the tourism sector. Presentation to the World Trade Organization's tourism symposium, 22-23 February. Retrieved 2 August 2005, from http://www.wto.org/spanish/tratop_s/serv_s/thailand.doc.

Ohmae, K. (1995). The end of the nation-state: The rise of regional economies. London: Harper Collins.

Oxfam International. (2002). Rigged rules and double standards: Trade, globalisation and he fight against poverty. New York: Oxfam International.

Patullo, P. (1996). Last resorts: The cost of tourism in the Caribbean. London: Casell.

Pleumarom, A. (no date a). Weighing the GATS on a development scale: the case of tourism in Goa. An edited article from the Tourism Investigation and Monitoring Team of the larger report from Equations (2002). Weighing the GATS on a development scale: the case of tourism in Goa, India. Retrieved 02 August 2005, from http://www.twnside.org.sg/title2/ttcd/EG-06.doc.

Pleumarom, A. (no date b). Campaign on corporate power in tourism. Clearinghouse for reviewing ecotourism, No. 1, Third World Network. Retrieved 12 August 2005, from http://www.twnside.org.sg/title/eco1.htm.

Pleumarom, A. (1999a). Eco-tourism: An ecological and economic trap for Third World countries. Third World Network. Retrieved 28 July 2003, from http://www.twnside.org.sg/title/cbd.htm.

Pleumarom, A. (1999b). Foreign takeover of Thailand's tourism industry: The other face of liberalization. Third World Network Briefing Paper for CSD7, No. 2. Retrieved 2 October 2002, from http://www.twnside.org.sg/title/takeover.htm.

Pleumarom, A. (1999c). The hidden costs of the 'new' tourisms – a focus on biopiracy. Third World Briefing Paper for CSD7, No. 1, Third World Network. Retrieved 28 July 2003, from http://www.twnside.org.sg/title/hidden.htm.

Pleumarom, A. (1999d). Tourism, globalisation and sustainable development. *Third World Resurgence*, 103, 4-8.

Pleumarom, A. (2000). Do we need an International Year of Ecotourism? Retrieved 4 April 2004, from http://www.twnside.org.sg/title/iye1.htm.

Reid, D. G. (2003). *Tourism, globalization and development*. London: Pluto Press.

Rethinking Tourism Project. (2000). Letter to Oliver Hillel, Tourism Programme Coordinator, UNEP. Retrieved 4 September 2004, from http://www.twnside.org.sg/title/ iye4.htm.

Richter, L. (1989). *The politics of tourism in Asia.* Honolulu: University of Hawaii Press.

Ritzer, G. (1996). *The McDonaldization of society.* Thousand Oaks, CA: Pine Forge Press.

Robertson, R. (1992). Globalization: Social theory and global culture. London: Sage.

Rosenau, J. N. (1996).The adaptation of the United Nations in a turbulent world. In R. Thukur (Ed.). *The United Nations at fifty: Retrospect and prospect* (pp. 229-224). Dunedin: University of Otago Press.

Rothkopf, D. (1997). In praise of cultural imperialism? Effects of globalization on culture. *Foreign Policy, 107,* 38-54.

Said, E. (1978). *Orientalism.* London: Penguin Books.

Scheuerman, W. (2002). Globalization. In E. N. Zalta (Ed.). *The Stanford Encyclopedia of Philosophy* (Fall 2002 edition). Retrieved 31 March 2003, from http://plato.stanford.edu/archives/fall2002/entries/globalization

Schivelbusch, W. (1986). The railway journey: trains and travel in the nineteenth century. Oxford: Blackwell.

Scholte, J. A. (2000). *Globalization: A critical introduction.* Houndmills, UK: Macmillan.

Sharma, D. (2005). The tsunami and the mangroves. *Dollars and Sense: The Magazine of Economic Justice, 260,* July/August. Retrieved 16 September 2005, from http://www.dollarsandsense.org/0705nesiah.html.

Sharpley, R. (2000a). Soft tourism. In J. Jafari (Ed.). *Encyclopedia of tourism* (p. 547). London: Routledge.

Sinclair, J., Jacka, E. and Cunningham, S. (2000). Peripheral vision. In F. J. Lechner and J. Boli (Eds.). *Globalization reader* (pp. 301-306). Oxford: Blackwell Publishers.

Sinclair, K. (2003). 'Cheap' move irks Hong Kong. *Travel Trade Gazette Asia,* July 25-31. . Retrieved 2 August 2005, from http://www.twnside.org.sg/title2/ttcd/EG-02.doc.

Sklair, L. (1991). *Sociology of the global system.* Baltimore: John Hopkins University Press.

Sklair, L. (1994). Capitalism and development in global perspective. In L. Sklair (Ed.). *Capitalism and development* (pp. 165-185). London: Routledge.

Sklair, L. (2002). *Globalization, capitalism and its alternatives.* Oxford: Oxford University Press.

Sub-resolution on the UN IYE-2002. (2001). Petition by the participants at National Conference on Human Rights, Social Movements, Globalization and the Law at Panchgani, India, 5 April. . In Rethinking Tourism Project. *An*

Indigenous and global south perspective on the International Year of Ecotourism: Voices of the marginalized by the IYE celebration (2002). Retrieved 4 April 2004, from

Thibault, D. (2004, 28 December). Media linking killer tsunami to global warming. CNSNews.com. Retrieved 16 September 2005, from http://www.cnsnews.com/ ViewNation.asp?Page=%5CNation%5Carchive%5C200412%5CNAT200412 28a.html.

Todaro, M. P. (1997). *Economic development*. London: Longman.

Tourism Concern. (2002). GATS and the tourism industry. *Fair Trade in Tourism Bulletin*, 3, Winter 2001/Spring 2002. Retrieved 2 August 2005, from http://www.tourismconcern.org.uk/downloads/pdfs/gats-and-tourism.pdf.

Tourism Interventions Group. (2004). Who really benefits from tourism? Statement of Concern at the 4th WSF. Retrieved 4 April 2005, from http://www.e-alliance.ch/media/media-4589.doc.

Tourism Investigation and Monitoring Team. (no date a). Thailand's case. Retrieved 9 September 2004, from http://www.twnside.org.sg/title/iye7.htm.

Tourism Investigation and Monitoring Team. (no date b). 2002: International year of reviewing ecotourism. In Rethinking Tourism Project. *An Indigenous and global south perspective on the International Year of Ecotourism: Voices of the marginalized by the IYE celebration* (2002). Retrieved 4 April 2004, from http://www.tourismrights.org/ documents/IYE%20Dossier.pdf.

Trask, H. K. (1993). Environmental racism in Hawai'i and the Pacific Basin. *ZMag,* Speech at University of Colorado at Boulder, 29 September. Retrieved 22 April 2003, from http://www.zmag.org/ZMag/articles/bartrask.htm.

United Nations Conference on Trade and Development. (no date). Competition and competitiveness in travel and tourism. Retrieved 17 August 2005, from http://tourism.unctad.org/QuickPlace/sustainable-tourism-for-development/Main.nsf/h_Index/D5D8B673628CAE9FC1256DFB0051B178/ ?OpenDocument.

United Nations Economic and Social Council. (1998). Declaring the year 2002 as the International Year of Ecotourism, Res. 1998/40. Retrieved 30 April 2004, from http://www.un.org/documents/ecosoc/res/1998/eres1998-40.htm.

United Nations World Tourism Organization. (no date a). About the World Tourism Organization. Retrieved 1 September 2004, from http://www.world-tourism.org/aboutwto/eng/menu.html.

United Nations World Tourism Organization. (no date b). Tourism 2020 vision. Retrieved 3 June 2005, from http://www.world-tourism.org/facts/eng/vision.htm.

United Nations World Tourism Organization. (no date c). What we offer? Retrieved 29 April 1998, from http://www.world-tourism.org/Offer.htm#Mision.

United Nations World Tourism Organization. (2002a). Green light for the transformation of WTO into a specialized agency of the United Nations. Retrieved 3 July 2004, from http://www.world-tourism.org/aboutwto/eng/menu.html.

United Nations World Tourism Organization. (2002b). *Tourism and poverty alleviation*. Madrid: UNWTO.

United Nations World Tourism Organization. (2003a). World Tourism Organization pushes for liberalization of trade with poor countries. Retrieved 2 August 2005, from http://www.world-tourism.org/newsroom/Releases/2003/December/liberalization.htm.

United Nations World Tourism Organization. (2003b). WTO urges Nigeria to embrace tourism. Retrieved 4 April 2004, from http://www.world-tourism.org/step/step/WTO%20Urges%20Nigeria%20to%20Embrace%20Tourism.pdf.

United Nations World Tourism Organization. (2004). Tourism enriches: A global communications campaign for tourism. Retrieved 10 December 2004, from http://www.world-tourism.org/newsroom/campaign/menu.htm.

United Nations World Tourism Organization and George Washington University. (2004). Washington declaration on tourism as a sustainable development strategy. Retrieved 12 December 2004, from http://www.world-tourism.org/education/PDF/ policy_forum/ WTO-TPF%20Declaration%20Final.2.efayos.pdf.

Vellas, F. and Becherel, L. (1995). *International tourism: An economic perspective*. Houndmills, UK: Macmillan Business.

Vivanco, L. (2001). The International Year of Ecotourism in an age of uncertainty. University of Vermont Environmental Symposium, October. In Rethinking Tourism Project. *An Indigenous and global south perspective on the International Year of Ecotourism: Voices of the marginalized by the IYE celebration* (2002). Retrieved 4 April 2004, from http://www.tourismrights.org/documents/IYE%20Dossier.pdf .

Vivanco, L. (2002). The Truth behind the International Year of Ecotourism. *The Ecologist*, 22 February. Retrieved 28 July 2003, from http://www.theecologist.org/archive_article. html?article=291.

Von Laue, T. (1987). *The world revolution of westernization*. New York: Oxford University Press.

Wahab, S. and Cooper, C. (2001a). Tourism, globalisation and the competitive advantage of nations. In S. Wahab and C. Cooper (Eds.). *Tourism in the age of globalisation* (pp. 3-21). London: Routledge.

Wahab, S. and Cooper, C. (Eds.). (2001b). *Tourism in the age of globalisation.* London: Routledge.

Waters, M. (1995). *Globalization.* London: Routledge.

Wheeller, B. (1991). Tourism's troubled times: Responsible tourism is not the answer. *Tourism Management,* 12(2), 91-96.

Whiteleg, J. and Fitz-Gibbon, S. (2003). Aviation's economic downside. Retrieved 16 September 2005, from http://www.greenparty.org.uk/files/reports/2004/AED3.htm.

Williams, M. (2002). The political economy of tourism, liberalization, gender and GATS. Occasional paper series on gender, trade and development. Retrieved 16 April 2004, from http://www.igtn.org/pdfs/30_TourismGATS.pdf.

Wiseman, J. (1997). Breaking the spell? Alternative responses to globalisation. In J. Wiseman (Ed.). *Alternatives to globalisation: An Asia-Pacific perspective.* Fitzroy, VIC: Community Aid Abroad.

World Bank. (2005). Madagascar: World Bank approves US$129 Million for integrated growth poles in Madagascar. Retrieved 2 August 2005, from http://web.worldbank.org/WBSITE/EXTERNAL/COUNTRIES/AFRICAEX T/MADAGASCAREXTN/0,,contentMDK:20579808~menuPK:356358~page PK:141137~piPK:141127~theSitePK:356352,00.html.

World Bank News. (1998). Bank revisits role of tourism in development, 7(12), 5.

World Economic Forum. (no date). About us. Retrieved 2 August 2005, from http://www.weforum.org/site/homepublic.nsf/Content/About+the+Forum+Su bhome.

World Social Forum. (2004). World Social Forum 2004. Retrieved 3 April 2005, from http://www.wsfindia.org/whoweare.php.

World Social Forum - Tourism. (2004). Tourism - a search for equitable options. Retrieved 24 December 2004, from http://www.wsf-tourism.org/home.asp

World Tourism Organization Business Council. (no date). What is the Business Council? Retrieved 2 August 2005, from http://www.world-tourism.org/members/affiliate/ eng/about_bus.htm.

World Trade Organization. (no date). The General Agreement on Trade in Services (GATS): Objectives, coverage and disciplines. Retrieved 7 July 2005, from http://www.wto.org/english/tratop_e/serv_e/gatsqa_e.htm#4.

World Trade Organization. (2001). WTO addresses developing country concerns in tourism symposium. Retrieved 6 July 2004, from http://www.wto.org/english/tratop_e/serv_e/symp_tourism_serv_feb01_e.htm.

World Travel and Tourism Council. (no date a). World Travel and Tourism Council. Retrieved 2 July 2006, from http://www.wttc.org.

World Travel and Tourism Council. (no date b). WTTC- The organisation. Retrieved 26 July 1999, from http://www.wttc.org.

World Travel and Tourism Council. (2002). Corporate social leadership in travel and tourism. Retrieved 14 September 2003, from http://www.wttc.org/publications/pdf/ CSLREPORT.pdf.

World Travel and Tourism Council. (2003). WTTC's blueprint for new tourism calls on government and industry to make significant long term commitments. Retrieved 2 August 2005, from http://www.wttc.org/frameset1.htm.

World Travel and Tourism Council. (2005a). Progress and priorities 2005/06. Retrieved 2 August 2005, from http://www.wttc.org.

World Travel and Tourism Council. (2005b). Travel and tourism: Sowing the seeds of economic growth. Retrieved 2 August 2005, from http://www.wttc.org/2005tsa/pdf/ Executive%20Summary%202005.pdf.

Worldwide Fund for Nature. (2001). Preliminary assessment of social and environmental effects of liberalisation in tourism services. WWF International Discussion Paper. Retrieved 2 September 2005, from http://www.icrtourism.org/Publications/tourism.PDF.

INDEX

D

E

F

I

T

U